M000280498

Birds of Arizona

Todd Telander

FALCONGUIDES

GUILFORD, CONNECTICUT
HELENA, MONTANA

AN IMPRINT OF GLOBE PEQUOT PRESS

To my wife, Kirsten, my children, Miles and Oliver, and my parents, all of whom have supported and encouraged me through the years. Special thanks to Mike Denny for his expert critique of the illustrations.

To buy books in quantity for corporate use or incentives, call **(800) 962-0973** or e-mail **premiums@GlobePequot.com**.

MIX
Paper from responsible sources
FSC
www.fsc.org
FSC® C005010

FALCONGUIDES®

FalconGuides is an imprint of Globe Pequot Press.
Falcon Field Guides is a trademark and Falcon, FalconGuides, and Outfit Your Mind are registered trademarks of Morris Book Publishing, LLC.

Illustrations: Todd Telander
Project editor: Julie Marsh
Text design: Sheryl P. Kober
Layout: Sue Murray

Library of Congress Cataloging-in-Publication Data is available on file.
ISBN 978-0-7627-7416-6
Printed in the United States of America

10 9 8 7 6 5 4 3 2 1

Contents

Passerines

Introduction

Arizona is an arid, landlocked state that consists of a great variety of habitats. To the north are high plateaus and canyons, including the Grand Canyon, that support vast ponderosa pine and juniper-pinyon woodlands; to the south is the mostly barren system of mountain ranges and basins, where desert shrub is found; and the mid-state is rugged country of the transitional zone between north and south, where rugged southern slopes support chaparral. This geographic diversity, with its accompanying array of climatic and vegetative zones, provides for an incredible number and variety of bird species. Arizona supports habitat for resident breeders and seasonal visitors, as well as those birds passing through on migration to and from South America and Canada. Although Arizona is home to or visited by over 500 species of birds, this guide describes the most common birds you are likely to encounter here and includes some that are only found in this area within the United States, like the Elegant Trogon and the Arizona Woodpecker.

Notes about the Species Accounts

Order
The order of species listed in this guide is based on the most recent version of the *Check-List of North American Birds,* published by the American Ornithologists' Union. The arrangement of some groups, especially within the nonpasserines, may be slightly different than that of older field guides but reflects the most recent accepted arrangement.

Names
Both the common name and the scientific name are included for each entry. Since common names tend to vary regionally, or there may be more than one common name for each species, the universally accepted scientific name of genus and species (such as *Pyrocephalus rubinus,* for the Vermilion Flycatcher) is more reliable to be certain of identification. Also, one can often learn interesting facts about a bird by the English translation of its Latin name. For instance, the generic name, *Pyrocephalus,* derives from the latin *pyro,* meaning fire, and *cephalus,* meaning head, describing the fire-red plumage on the head of this flycatcher.

Families
Birds are grouped into families based on similar traits, behaviors, and genetics. When trying to identify an unfamiliar bird, it can often be helpful to first place it into a family, which will reduce your search to a smaller group. For example, if you see a long-legged, long-billed bird lurking in the shallows, you can begin by looking in the family group of Ardeidae (Herons, Egrets), and narrow your search from there.

Size
The size given for each bird is the average length from the tip of the bill to the end of the tail if the bird was laid out flat. Sometimes females and males vary in size, and this variation is described in the

text. Size can be misleading if you are looking at a small bird that happens to have a very long tail or bill. It can be more effective to judge the bird's relative size by comparing the size difference between two or more species.

Season

The season given in the accounts is the time when the greatest number of individual birds occurs in Arizona. Some species are year-round residents that breed here. Others may spend only summers or winters here, and some may be transient, only stopping during the spring or fall migration. Even if only part of the year is indicated for a species, be aware that there may be individuals that arrive earlier or remain for longer than the given time frame. Plumage also changes with the season for many birds, and this is indicated in the text and illustrations.

Habitat

A bird's habitat is one of the first clues to its identification. Note the environment where you see a bird and compare it with the description listed. This can be especially helpful when identifying a bird that shares traits with related species. For example, Snowy Egrets and Cattle Egrets are similar in appearance, but Snowy Egrets are found near water while Cattle Egrets frequent upland fields and pastures.

Illustrations

The illustrations show the adult bird in the plumage most likely to be encountered during the season(s) it is in Arizona. If it is likely that you will find more than one type of plumage during this time, the alternate plumage is also shown. For birds that are sexually dimorphic (females and males look different), illustrations of both sexes are usually included. Other plumages, such as those of juveniles and alternate morphs, are described in the text.

Bird Topography and Terms

Bird topography describes the outer surface of a bird and how various anatomical structures fit together. Below is a diagram outlining the terms most commonly used to describe the feathers and bare parts of a bird.

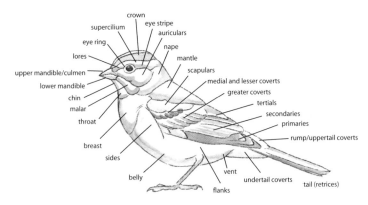

NONPASSERINES

Canada Goose,
Branta canadensis
Family Anatidae (Ducks, Geese)
Size: 27–35"
Season: Winter
Habitat: Marshes, grasslands, public parks, golf courses

The Canada Goose is the state's most common goose and is found in suburban settings. It is vegetarian, foraging on land for grass, seeds, and grain, or in the water by upending like the dabbling ducks. It has a heavy body with short, thick legs and a long neck. Overall its coloring is barred gray brown with a white rear, short black tail, black neck, and a white patch running under the neck to behind the eye. During the goose's powerful flight, the white rump makes a semicircular patch between the tail and back. Voice is a loud honk. In flight Canada Geese form the classic V-formation. The adult is illustrated.

Gadwall, *Anas strepera*
Family Anatidae (Ducks, Geese)
Size: 20.5"
Season: Winter; year-round in north-central Arizona
Habitat: Shallow lakes, marshes

The Gadwall is a buoyant, plain-colored dabbling duck with a steep forehead and a somewhat angular head. The breeding male is grayish overall with very fine variegation and barring. The rump and undertail coverts are black, the scapulars are light orange brown, the tertials are gray, and the head is lighter below the eye and darker above. Females and nonbreeding males are mottled brownish, with few distinguishing markings. In flight there is a distinctive white speculum that is most prominent in males. Gadwalls dabble or dive for a variety of aquatic plants and invertebrates, and often gather in large flocks away from the shore. The breeding female (top) and breeding male (bottom) are illustrated.

DUCKS, GEESE

American Wigeon, *Anas americana*
Family Anatidae (Ducks, Geese)
Size: 19"
Season: Winter
Habitat: Shallow ponds, fields

The American Wigeon is also known as the Baldpate, in reference to its white crown. A wary and easily alarmed duck, it feeds on the water's surface, often gleaning prey stirred up by the efforts of diving ducks. The underside is a light cinnamon color with white undertail coverts, and the back is light brown. The male has a white crown and forehead with a very slight crest when seen in profile, and a glossy dark green patch extending from the eye to the back of the neck. A white wing covert patch can usually be seen on the folded wing but is more obvious in flight. The head of the female is unmarked and brownish. The breeding female (top) and breeding male (bottom) are illustrated.

Mallard, *Anas platyrhynchos*
Family Anatidae (Ducks, Geese)
Size: 23"
Season: Year-round
Habitat: Virtually any water environment, parks, urban areas

The ubiquitous Mallard is the most abundant duck in the Northern Hemisphere. It is a classic dabbling duck, plunging its head into the water with its tail up, searching for aquatic plants, animals, and snails, although it will also eat worms, seeds, insects, and even mice. Noisy and quacking, it is heavy but is a strong flier. The male has a dark head with green or blue iridescence, a white neck ring, and a large yellow bill. The underparts are pale with a chestnut-brown breast. The female is plain brownish with buff scalloped markings and has a dark eye line and an orangey bill with a dark center. The speculum is blue on both sexes, and the tail coverts often curl upward. Mallards form huge floating flocks called "rafts." To achieve flight, the duck lifts straight into the air without running. The breeding female (top) and breeding male (bottom) are illustrated.

3

Blue-winged Teal,
Anas discors
Family Anatidae (Ducks, Geese)
Size: 16"
Season: Summer
Habitat: Freshwater marshes and mudflats, wet agricultural areas

The Blue-winged Teal, also known as the White-faced Teal, is a small duck that skims the water surface for aquatic plants and invertebrates, often forming large flocks. The male is mottled brown below, with a prominent white patch near the hip area, and is dark above, with gray on the head and a white vertical crescent at the base of the bill. The female is brownish with scalloped flanks, a plain head with a dark eye line, and pale lores. Both sexes have a light blue wing patch visible in flight. The breeding female (top) and breeding male (bottom) are illustrated.

Northern Shoveler,
Anas clypeata
Family Anatidae (Ducks, Geese)
Size: 19"
Season: Winter
Habitat: Shallow marshes, lakes, bays

Also known as the Spoonbill Duck, the Northern Shoveler skims the surface of the water with its neck extended, scooping up aquatic animals and plants with its long, spatulate bill. It also sucks up the ooze from mud and strains it through bristles at the edge of its bill, retaining worms, leeches, and snails. This medium-size duck seems top-heavy due to its large bill. Plumage in the male is white beneath, with a large chestnut side patch, and it has a dark green head and gray bill. The female is pale brownish overall with an orangey bill. The breeding female (top) and breeding male (bottom) are illustrated.

Cinnamon Teal, *Anas cyanoptera*
Family Anatidae (Ducks, Geese)
Size: 16"
Season: Year-round in southern
Arizona; summer elsewhere
Habitat: Marshes, shallow lakes

The Cinnamon Teal is a small dabbling duck with a wide, spatulate bill. The breeding male is cinnamon brown overall with darker hindquarters and paler, sharply shaped back feathers. The eye is golden red and the bill is dark gray. Females and nonbreeding males are a paler shade of cinnamon with scalloped plumage and closely resemble the Blue-winged Teal. In flight the blue inner wing patch and white underwing are visible. Cinnamon Teals dabble in shallow water for plant material, insects, and aquatic invertebrates, filtering mud through their wide bills. The breeding male (bottom) and female (top) are illustrated.

Northern Pintail, *Anas acuta*
Family Anatidae (Ducks, Geese)
Size: 21"
Season: Winter
Habitat: Marshes, shallow lakes,
coastal bays

Among the most abundant ducks in North America, the Northern Pintail is an elegant, slender dabbling duck with a long neck, small head, and narrow wings. In breeding plumage the male has long, pointed central tail feathers. It is gray along the back and sides, with a brown head and a white breast. A white stripe extends from the breast along the back of the neck. The female is mottled brown and tan overall with a light brown head. To feed, the Northern Pintail bobs its head into the water to capture aquatic invertebrates and plants from the muddy bottom. It rises directly out of the water to take flight. The breeding female (top) and breeding male (bottom) are illustrated.

Green-winged Teal,

Anas crecca
Family Anatidae (Ducks, Geese)
Size: 14"
Season: Winter
Habitat: Marshes, ponds

The Green-winged Teal is a cute, very small, active duck with a small, thin bill. The breeding male is silvery gray with a dotted tawny breast patch, a pale yellow hip patch, and a distinct vertical white bar on its side. The head is rusty brown with an iridescent green patch around and behind the eye. Females and nonbreeding males are mottled brown with a dark eye line and white belly. Green-winged Teals dabble in the shallows for plant material and small invertebrates. They are quick and agile in flight and sport a bright green speculum. They form very large winter flocks. The breeding female (top) and breeding male (bottom) are illustrated.

Redhead, *Aythya americana*
Family Anatidae (Ducks, Geese)
Size: 19"
Season: Winter; year-round in northeastern Arizona
Habitat: Shallow lakes, marshes

The Redhead is a heavy-bodied diving duck with a steep forehead and a large, rounded head. The breeding male is pale gray with a dark rear end and breast. The head is light rusty brown, the eye is yellow, and the bill is bluish with a black tip. The female is brownish gray overall with pale areas at the base of the bill and throat. In both sexes the upper side of the wing has white flight feathers and dark gray coverts. These birds "run" across the water to become airborne. They forage by diving for aquatic plants and invertebrates, and may form huge floating "rafts" during the winter. Redheads are similar in pattern to the larger Canvasbacks. The breeding female (top) and breeding male (bottom) are illustrated.

Ring-necked Duck, *Aythya collaris*
Family Anatidae (Ducks, Geese)
Size: 17"
Season: Winter
Habitat: Shallow lakes and ponds near woodlands, coastal bays

The Ring-necked Duck, also known as the Ring-billed Duck, is in the group of diving ducks that typically swim underwater to find plant and animal prey, although it may also behave like a dabbling duck and bob for food at the surface. This gregarious small duck looks tall, with its postlike head and neck and a peaked crown. The breeding male is stunning, with contrasting light and dark plumage and a dark metallic brown-purple head. The bill is gray with a white ring and black tip, and the base of the bill is edged with white feathers. The female is more brownish overall with a white eye ring. The ring around the neck, for which this duck is named, is actually a very inconspicuous brownish band at the bottom of the neck in the male bird. The breeding female (top) and breeding male (bottom) are illustrated.

Lesser Scaup, *Aythya affinis*
Family Anatidae (Ducks, Geese)
Size: 17"
Season: Winter
Habitat: Marshes, shallow lakes, coastal bays

The Lesser Scaup is a small, short-bodied duck with a tall head profile and a relatively thin bill. The breeding male is distinctly two-toned, with white sides, a variegated pale gray back, and a black rear and front. The head has a dark metallic violet or greenish cast in good light, and the bill has a small black dot at the nail. The nonbreeding male is paler with brown on the sides. Females are gray brown with a dark brown head and a white patch at the base of the bill. This is a diving duck that forages for aquatic plants and insects. It is very similar to the Greater Scaup, but is smaller and has a more peaked head. The breeding female (top) and breeding male (bottom) are illustrated.

Bufflehead, *Bucephala albeola*
Family Anatidae (Ducks, Geese)
Size: 14"
Season: Winter
Habitat: Lakes, rivers, coastal bays

The Bufflehead is a diminutive diving duck; indeed, it is the smallest duck in North America. Also known as the Bumblebee Duck, it forms small flocks that forage in the open water for aquatic plants and invertebrates. The puffy, rounded head seems large for the body and compared to the small gray-blue bill. The breeding male is striking, with a large white patch on the back half of its head that contrasts with the black front of the head and back. The underside is white. The female is paler overall with a dark gray-brown head and an airfoil-shaped white patch behind the eye. Flight is low to the water, with rapid wing beats. The breeding female (top) and breeding male (bottom) are illustrated.

DUCKS, GEESE

Common Goldeneye,
Bucephala clangula
Family Anatidae (Ducks, Geese)
Size: 18.5"
Season: Winter
Habitat: Lakes, rivers

The Common Goldeneye is a compact, large-headed diving duck with a tall, rounded head and a stubby bill. The breeding male is plumed in stark black and white; it has a white body with thin black streaks above and a black head and rear end. It has bright yellow eyes and a circular white patch between the eye and the bill. The female is gray overall with a brown head and a yellow-tipped bill. This duck is sometimes called the "Whistler" because of the whistling sound made by its wings in flight. It forms small flocks in the winter. The breeding male (bottom) and female (top) are illustrated.

Common Merganser,
Mergus merganser
Family Anatidae (Ducks, Geese)
Size: 25"
Season: Winter; year-round in central Arizona
Habitat: Lakes near woodlands, rivers, coastal areas

Mergansers are known as Fishing Ducks or Sawtooths. They dive and chase fish of considerable size underwater and secure their catch with a long, thin bill that is serrated along the edges. Both male and female Red-breasted Mergansers sport a fine, long two-part crest. The male has a white band around the neck, a dark head, a red bill, and gray flanks. The female is grayish overall with a brown head. The nonbreeding male closely resembles the female. Flight is low and quick on pointed wings. The breeding female (top) and breeding male (bottom) are illustrated.

Red-breasted Merganser,
Mergus serrator
Family Anatidae (Ducks, Geese)
Size: 23"
Season: Year-round
Habitat: Lakes near woodlands, rivers

Like the common Merganser, the Red-breasted Merganser is a member of the Fishing Ducks or Sawtooths. They dive and chase fish of considerable size underwater and secure their catches with long, thin bills that are serrated along the edges. Both male and female Red-breasted Mergansers sport a fine, long two-part crest. The male has a white band around its neck, a dark head, red bill, and gray flanks. The female is grayish overall with a brown head. The nonbreeding male closely resembles the female. Flight is low and quick on pointed wings. The breeding male (left) and female (right) are illustrated.

Ruddy Duck, *Oxyura jamaicencis*
Family Anatidae (Ducks, Geese)
Size: 15"
Season: Year-round
Habitat: Open water, wetlands, bays

The Ruddy Duck is a member of the "stiff-tailed ducks," known for their rigid tail feathers that are often cocked up in display. It dives deep into the water for its food, which consists of aquatic vegetation, and flies low over the water with quick wing beats. It is a relatively small duck with a big head and a flat, broad body. The breeding male is rich sienna brown overall with white cheeks, a black cap and nape, and a bright blue bill. The female is drab with a conspicuous dark stripe across the cheek. Nonbreeding males become gray. The Ruddy Duck can sink low into the water, grebe-like, and often dives to escape danger. The breeding female (top) and breeding male (bottom) are illustrated.

Scaled Quail, *Callipepla squamata*
Family Odontophoridae (Quail)
Size: 10"
Season: Year-round
Habitat: Dry, open grasslands and scrub

Also known as the Cottontop, the Scaled Quail is a plump, short-tailed ground bird with a tall, white-tipped crest. The upperparts and head are gray brown, while the underparts and around the neck are paler with black-tipped feathers that create a scaled appearance. There is also white streaking along the flanks and the back edges of the tertials. Females generally have a shorter crest. Scaled Quail forage on the ground in large groups, or coveys, for insects and grains, and they usually run away rather than fly when alarmed. The voice is a two-part clucking *pe-cos*, or a short shriek. The adult male is illustrated.

Gambel's Quail,
Callipepla gambelii
Family Odontophoridae (Quail)
Size: 10.5"
Season: Year-round
Habitat: Dry scrublands, riparian areas

The Gambel's Quail is a plump, short-legged ground bird with a small head and a curious, forward-projecting head plume and a short bill. The male is gray overall with white barring along the rufous sides and flanks, with a tan belly surrounding a black, circular patch. The head is boldly marked with a rufous crown, black face, and white stripes above the eyes and down the face. The female has a pale gray head with a much smaller plume, and no black patch on the belly. Gambel's Quail travel in large coveys, searching the ground for insects and seeds, and often roost near a water source. The voice is a short, dry *sit-sit*, or a nasal *cha CA go*, repeated several times. The adult male is illustrated.

Wild Turkey, *Meleagris gallopavo*
Family Phasianidae (Pheasants, Grouse, Turkeys)
Size: 36–48", male larger than female
Season: Year-round
Habitat: Open mixed woodlands

The Wild Turkey is a very large (though slimmer than the domestic variety), dark ground-dwelling bird. The legs are thick and stout, and the heavily barred plumage is quite iridescent in strong light. The head and neck appear small for the body size and are covered with bluish, warty, crinkled bare skin that droops under the chin in a red wattle. Often foraging in flocks, turkeys roam the ground for seeds, grubs, and insects and then roost at night in trees. Males emit the familiar *gobble*, while females are less vocal, making a soft clucking sound. In display the male hunches with its tail up and spread like a giant fan. Southwestern races, as in Texas, show white banding on the tail and uppertail coverts. The adult male is illustrated.

Eared Grebe, *Podiceps nigricollis*
Family Podicipedidae (Grebes)
Size: 13"
Season: Winter
Habitat: Shallow freshwater ponds and lakes

The Eared Grebe is a small, thin grebe with a narrow, pointed bill that turns up at the tip. The breeding adult has a black head, neck, and back, a pale belly, and rufous sides. The head has a peaked crown, bright red eyes, and golden-yellow ear tufts. In winter the birds have whitish head markings, breast, and sides, with no ear tufts. A clean, white secondary patch can be seen on the wing in flight. The tail is tiny and hidden. Eared Grebes are gregarious, forming large nesting colonies, and forage by diving for aquatic invertebrates and insects. They are slightly more buoyant than other grebes. The breeding adult is illustrated.

GREBES

Western Grebe,
Aechmophorus occidentalis
Family Podicipedidae (Grebes)
Size: 25"
Season: Year-round
Habitat: Shallow freshwater ponds and lakes

The Western Grebe is a large, elegant grebe with an extremely long, thin neck and a long, pointed greenish-yellow bill with an upturned lower mandible. It is slate gray above and crisp white below. The head and neck are cleanly divided in black and white, with black encompassing the red eye (unlike the similar Clark's Grebe). Western Grebes dive for fish and aquatic invertebrates, and voice a high-pitched, rattling *kreek-kreek*. They rarely take flight, but do so following a long, labored run across the water surface. This grebe was once considered the same species as the Clark's Grebe. The breeding adult is illustrated.

Pied-billed Grebe,
Podilymbus podiceps
Family Podicipedidae (Grebes)
Size: 13"
Season: Year-round
Habitat: Freshwater ponds and lakes

The Pied-billed Grebe is a secretive, small grebe that lurks in sheltered waters, diving for small fish, leeches, snails, and crawfish. When alarmed, or to avoid predatory snakes and hawks, it has the habit of sinking until only its head is above water, remaining that way until danger has passed. It is brownish overall and slightly darker above with a tiny tail and short wings. The breeding adult has a conspicuous dark ring around the middle of the bill, which is missing in winter plumage. Pied-billed Grebes nest on a floating mat of vegetation. The breeding adult is illustrated.

Double-crested Cormorant,
Phalacrocorax auritus
Family Phalacrocoracidae (Cormorants)
Size: 32"
Season: Year-round
Habitat: Open waters

Named for the two long white plumes that emerge from behind the eyes during breeding season, the Double-crested Cormorant is an expert swimmer that dives underwater to chase down fish. Because its plumage lacks the normal oils to repel water, it stands with wings outstretched to dry itself. It is all black with a pale glossy cast on the back and wings. The eyes are bright green, the bill is thin and hooked, and the throat patch and lores are yellow. The breeding adult is illustrated.

American White Pelican,
Pelecanus erythrorhynchos
Family Pelecanidae (Pelicans)
Size: 62"
Season: Winter in southwestern Arizona; spring and fall migrant elsewhere
Habitat: Open freshwater

One of North America's largest birds, the American White Pelican has a wingspan of over 9 feet. It is white overall with black flight feathers. The massive bill is orange and has a membranous, expandable throat pouch. In posture the bird holds its neck in a characteristic strong kink and its folded wings in a peak along its back. American White Pelicans often feed in cooperative groups, herding fish as they swim and scooping them up by dipping their bills in the water. They never plunge-dive like Brown Pelicans. When they are breeding, a strange horny growth appears on the upper mandible in both sexes. The nonbreeding adult is illustrated.

American Bittern,
Botaurus lentiginosus
Family Ardeidae (Herons, Egrets)
Size: 27"
Season: Winter
Habitat: Marshy areas with dense vegetation

The American Bittern is a fairly large, secretive heron with a small head, a long, straight bill, and a thick body. It has a habit of standing still with its neck and bill pointed straight up to imitate the surrounding reeds. Its plumage is very cryptic: Above it is variegated brown and tan, and below it is pale brown or whitish with thick rust-colored streaking that extends up the neck. The bill is yellow green and dark on the upper mandible. A dark patch extends from the lower bill to the upper neck. The legs are yellow green and thick. American Bitterns skulk slowly through reeds and grasses to catch frogs, insects, and invertebrates. The adult is illustrated.

Great Blue Heron,
Ardea herodias
Family Ardeidae (Herons, Egrets)
Size: 46"
Season: Year-round
Habitat: Most aquatic areas, including lakes, creeks, marshes

The Great Blue Heron is the largest heron in North America. Walking slowly through shallow water or fields, it stalks fish, crabs, and small vertebrates, catching them with its massive bill. With long legs and a long neck, it is blue gray overall with a white face and a heavy yellow-orange bill. The crown is black and supports plumes of medium length. The front of the neck is white with distinct black chevrons fading into breast plumes. In flight the neck is tucked back and the wing beats are regular and labored. The adult is illustrated.

Great Egret, *Ardea alba*
Family Ardeidae (Herons, Egrets)
Size: 38"
Season: Year-round in southwestern Arizona; spring and fall migrant elsewhere
Habitat: Freshwater and saltwater marshes

One of California's most widespread herons, the Great Egret is all white and has a long, thin yellow bill and long black legs. It develops long, lacy plumes across its back during the breeding season. Stalking slowly, it pursues fish, frogs, and other aquatic animals. The breeding adult is illustrated.

Snowy Egret,
Egretta thula
Family Ardeidae (Herons, Egrets)
Size: 24"
Season: Year-round in
southwestern Arizona; spring
and fall migrant elsewhere
Habitat: Open water, marshes,
swamps

The Snowy Egret is all white, with lacy plumes across the back in breeding season. The bill is slim and black, and the legs are black with bright yellow feet. The juvenile has greenish legs with a yellow stripe along the front. The Snowy Egret forages for fish and frogs along the shore by moving quickly, shuffling to stir up prey, which it then stabs with its bill. Sometimes it may run to pursue its prey. To recall the name of this bird, keep in mind that it wears yellow "boots" because it is cold or "snowy." The breeding adult is illustrated.

Green Heron, *Butorides virescens*
Family Ardeidae (Herons, Egrets)
Size: 18"
Season: Year-round
Habitat: Ponds, creeks, wetlands

The Green Heron is a compact, crow-size heron that perches on low branches over the water, crouching forward to search for fish, snails, and insects. It is known to toss a bug into the water to attract fish. The Green Heron is really not so green, but rather a dull grayish blue with a burgundy-chestnut neck and black crown. The bill is dark, and the legs are bright yellow orange. When disturbed, its crest feathers rise, and it stands erect and twitches its tail. It is fairly secretive and solitary. The adult is illustrated.

Black-crowned Night-Heron, *Nycticorax nycticorax*
Family Ardeidae (Herons, Egrets)
Size: 25"
Season: Year-round along the coast, summer inland
Habitat: Marshes, swamps with wooded banks

The nocturnal Black-crowned Night-Heron is a stocky, thick-necked heron with a comparatively large head and a sharp, heavy, thick bill. It has pale gray wings, white underparts, and a black crown, back, and bill. The eyes are piercing red, and the legs are yellow. There are thin, white plumes trailing from the back of the head, becoming longer during the breeding season. During the day it roosts in groups, but at night it forages alone, waiting motionless for prey such as fish or crabs. It may even raid the nests of other birds. Its voice is composed of low-pitched barks and croaks. The adult is illustrated.

White-faced Ibis, *Plegadis chihi*
Family Threskiornithidae (Ibises)
Size: 23"
Season: Winter in southwestern Arizona; spring and fall migrant elsewhere
Habitat: Swamps, shallows of freshwater lakes, fields

The White-faced Ibis is somewhat heronlike in shape with a relatively short neck and a long, down-curved grayish bill. The plumage is dark, metallic green black on the wings and back, with a dark chestnut body, neck, and head. The lores are reddish and bordered with white feathers that encircle the dark red eyes. In winter adults of both sexes are all dark with pale streaking on the head and neck, and they lack the white feathers around the eye. Breeding adults have bright red legs. Unlike herons, ibises fly with their necks extended. They walk steadily while picking and probing with their long bills for aquatic invertebrates, and they roost in trees. The breeding adult is illustrated.

Black Vulture,
Coragyps atratus
Family Cathartidae (New World Vultures)
Size: 25"
Season: Year-round
Habitat: Dry open country

Like the Turkey Vulture, the Black Vulture is adept at soaring. Its wing beats, however, are faster, and while soaring, it holds its wings at a flat angle instead of a dihedral. It is stocky in physique and has a short, stubby tail and shorter wings than the Turkey Vulture. The primaries are pale on an otherwise black body, and the head is bald and gray. The Black Vulture eats carrion and garbage and is quite aggressive at feeding sites. The adult is illustrated.

Turkey Vulture, *Cathartes aura*
Family Cathartidae (New World Vultures)
Size: 27"
Season: Year-round in southwestern Arizona; summer elsewhere
Habitat: Dry open country

The Turkey Vulture is known for its effortless, skilled soaring. It often soars for hours, without flapping, rocking in the breeze on 6-foot wings that form an upright V-shape or dihedral angle. It has a black body and inner wing with pale flight feathers and tail feathers that give it a noticeable two-toned appearance from below. The tail is longish, and the feet extend no more than halfway past the base of the tail. The head is naked, red, and small, so the bird appears almost headless in flight. The bill is strongly hooked to aid in tearing apart its favored prey, carrion. Juveniles have a dark gray head. Turkey Vultures often roost in flocks and form groups around food or at a roadkill site. The adult is illustrated.

Osprey, *Pandion haliaetus*
Family Pandionidae (Osprey)
Size: 23", female larger than male
Season: Year-round
Habitat: Always near water, salt or fresh

Also known as the Fish Hawk, the Osprey exhibits a dramatic feeding method, plunging feetfirst into the water to snag fish. Sometimes it completely submerges itself, then laboriously flies off with its heavy catch. It is dark brown above and white below, and has a distinct dark eye stripe contiguous with the nape. Females show a dark, mottled "necklace" across the breast, and juveniles have pale streaking on the back. The Osprey flies with an obvious crook at the wrist, appearing gull-like, and its wings are long and narrow with a dark carpal patch. The adult is illustrated.

Northern Harrier,
Circus cyaneus
Family Accipitridae (Hawks, Eagles)
Size: 18", female larger than male
Season: Winter
Habitat: Open fields, wetlands

Also known as the Marsh Hawk, the Northern Harrier flies low to the ground, methodically surveying its hunting grounds for rodents and other small animals. When it spots prey, aided by its acute hearing, it drops abruptly to the ground to attack. The Northern Harrier is a thin raptor with a long tail and long, flame-shaped wings that are broad in the middle. The face has a distinct owl-like facial disk, and there is a conspicuous white patch at the rump. Males are gray above with a white, streaked breast and black wing tips. Females are brown with a barred breast. The juvenile is similar in plumage to the female, but with a pale belly. The adult female (bottom) and male (top) are illustrated.

Bald Eagle,
Haliaeetus leucocephalus
Family Accipitridae (Hawks, Eagles)
Size: 30–40", female larger than male
Season: Year-round in central
Arizona; winter elsewhere
Habitat: Lakes, rivers with tall
perches or cliffs

The Bald Eagle is a large raptor that is widespread but fairly uncommon. It eats fish or scavenges dead animals, and congregates in large numbers where food is abundant. Its plumage is dark brown, contrasting with the white head and tail. Juveniles show white splotching across the wings and breast. The yellow bill is large and powerful, and the talons are large and sharp. In flight the eagle holds its wings fairly flat and straight, resembling a long plank. Bald Eagles make huge nests of sticks high in trees. The adult is illustrated.

Golden Eagle, *Aquila chrysaetos*
Family Accipitridae (Hawks, Eagles)
Size: 30", female larger than male
Season: Year-round
Habitat: Mountainous areas, hills,
open country

The Golden Eagle is a solitary, very large buteo-shaped raptor with large talons and long, broad wings with a 6½-foot wingspan. Its plumage is dark brown overall with a pale golden nape and a relatively small head. The bill is large and hooked and forms a wide gape. The juvenile shows a white patch at the base of the tail and at the base of the flight feathers. Golden Eagles hold their wings horizontal or with a very slight dihedral angle in flight. They forage from a perch or by soaring overhead, attacking mammals, reptiles, and birds. They may also eat carrion. The adult is illustrated.

Northern Goshawk,
Accipiter gentilis
Family Accipitridae (Hawks, Eagles)
Size: 22", female larger than male
Season: Year-round
Habitat: Woodlands, bushy areas

The Northern Goshawk is Colorado's largest accipiter, similar in shape to the Cooper's and Sharp-shinned Hawks, but often mistaken for a buteo because of its large size. It is dark gray on the back and finely barred white and gray underneath. The head has a white superciliary stripe bordered by a dark crown and ear patch. Juveniles are mottled brown with coarse streaking across the breast and have more noticeably banded tails. Northern Goshawks hunt from a perch, ambush-style, flying through woodlands to capture birds and mammals up to rabbit size. The adult is illustrated.

Sharp-shinned Hawk,
Accipiter striatus
Family Accipitridae (Hawks, Eagles)
Size: 10–14", female larger than male
Season: Year-round
Habitat: Woodlands, bushy areas

The Sharp-shinned Hawk is North America's smallest accipiter, with a longish, squared tail and stubby, rounded wings. Its short wings allow for agile flight in tight, wooded quarters, where it quickly attacks small birds in flight. It is grayish above and light below, barred with pale rufous stripes. The eyes are set forward on the face to aid in the direct pursuit of prey. The juvenile is white below, streaked with brown. The similar Cooper's Hawk is larger with a longer, rounded tail, and hunts more often in open country. The adult is illustrated.

Harris's Hawk,
Parabuteo unicinctus
Family Accipitridae (Hawks, Eagles)
Size: 20", female larger than male
Season: Year-round
Habitat: Arid open woodlands,
scrub, desert

The Harris's Hawk is a somewhat lanky buteo with a long tail and legs and a smallish head. It is dark brown overall with chestnut shoulders, underwing coverts, and thighs. The base of the tail is white above and below, and there is a white terminal band, forming a broad black band across the tail. Juveniles show pale streaking on the breast. Harris's Hawks hunt by coursing low over the ground, searching for mammals to rabbit-size, reptiles, and insects. They perch on poles and tall cacti, often in a horizontal posture. Their range extends into South America, where they are known as Bay-winged Hawks because of their broad, paddlelike wings. The adult is illustrated.

Red-tailed Hawk, *Buteo jamaicensis*
Family Accipitridae (Hawks, Eagles)
Size: 20"
Season: Year-round
Habitat: Open country, prairies

This widespread species is the most common buteo in the United States. It has broad, rounded wings and a stout, hooked bill. Its plumage is highly variable depending on geographic location. In general, the underparts are light with darker streaking that forms a dark band across the belly, the upperparts are dark brown, and the tail is rufous. Light spotting occurs along the scapulars. In flight there is a noticeable dark patch along the inner leading edge of the underwing. Red-tailed Hawks glide down from perches, such as telephone poles and posts in open country, to catch rodents, and they may also hover to spot prey. They are usually seen alone or in pairs. Voice is the familiar *keeer!* The western adult is illustrated.

Swainson's Hawk,
Buteo swainsoni
Family Accipitridae (Hawks, Eagles)
Size: 19", female larger than male
Season: Summer
Habitat: Dry prairies, open fields

The Swainson's Hawk is a buteo with a long tail, long wings with pointed tips, and a relatively small, rounded head. It has variable plumage colors, ranging from dark morphs to the more common light morphs. The light morph has a white underside, a dark brown back, a rufous breast, and white lores and chin. Darker forms become rufous or dark brown on the breast and belly. In flight the light morph has pale wing linings and a pale belly that contrasts with its darker flight feathers and tail. Swainson's Hawks feed on small mammals, insects, and reptiles, either descending from a perch or by stalking on the ground. The hawk's voice is a high-pitched *eeeeww*. The adult is illustrated.

Ferruginous Hawk,
Buteo regalis
Family Accipitridae (Hawks, Eagles)
Size: 23", female larger than male
Season: Year-round in northeastern Arizona; winter elsewhere
Habitat: Dry prairies, open country

The Ferruginous Hawk is Arizona's largest buteo. It has a thick body and neck, a large hooked bill, and long, broad wings. Two color morphs occur: light and dark. The light morph is white below with rufous barring on the flanks and thighs. The back is mottled brown and rufous with grayish flight feathers. The dark morph is dark brown overall with white on the undersides of the flight feathers and tail. Ferruginous Hawks stalk their prey of small mammals from a perch, or by hovering or soaring. The light morph adult is illustrated.

Crested Caracara,

Caracara cheriway
Family Falconidae (Falcons)
Size: 23"
Season: Year-round
Habitat: Dry prairies and scrubland of south-central Arizona

The Crested Caracara is a falcon that is somewhat vulturelike in its behavior. It forages on carcasses or immobile prey, which it finds by soaring on flat wings or cruising over pastures and open savanna. It may also perch on poles or on the ground. Its head seems large for its body and it has a long neck and long legs. It is an overall dark bird with a white neck, black cap, and large, hooked bill. The face has a large patch of reddish bare skin. In flight the white wing tips and tail are distinctive. This tropical falcon is rare in the United States and was once a threatened species here. The adult is illustrated.

American Kestrel,

Falco sparverius
Family Falconidae (Falcons)
Size: 10"
Season: Year-round
Habitat: Open country, urban areas

North America's most common falcon, the American Kestrel is a tiny, robin-size falcon with long, pointed wings and tail. Fast in flight, it hovers above fields or dives from its perch on a branch or a wire to capture small animals and insects. The upperparts are rufous and barred with black, the wings are blue gray, and the breast is buff or white and streaked with black spots. The head is patterned with a gray crown and vertical patches of black down the face. The female has rufous wings and a barred tail. Also known as the Sparrow Hawk, it has a habit of flicking its tail up and down while perched. The adult male is illustrated.

Peregrine Falcon,

Falco peregrinus
Family Falconidae (Falcons)
Size: 17"
Season: Year-round
Habitat: Open country, cliffs, urban areas

The Peregrine Falcon is a powerful and agile raptor with long, sharply pointed wings. It is dark slate gray above and pale whitish below with uniform barring below the breast. Plumage on the head forms a distinctive "helmet" with a white ear patch and chin contrasting with the blackish face and crown. Juveniles are mottled brown overall with heavy streaking on the underside. Peregrine Falcons attack other birds in flight using spectacular high-speed aerial dives. Once threatened by DDT pollution that caused thinning of their eggshells, Peregrine Falcons have made a dramatic comeback. The adult is illustrated.

Prairie Falcon,

Falco mexicanus
Family Falconidae (Falcons)
Size: 17", female larger than male
Season: Year-round
Habitat: Prairies, open land near cliffs and mountains

The Prairie Falcon is large, with a long tail and narrow, pointed wings. The body is pale brown gray above and white below with brown streaking. The head is patterned with a white ear patch and chin, a dark malar patch, and a large black eye. The underside in flight is marked with dark inner wing coverts and axillar (armpit) feathers. Prairie Falcons attack small animals on the ground from a perch or after aerial pursuit. The adult is illustrated.

Sora, *Porzana carolina*
Family Rallidae (Rails, Coots)
Size: 9"
Season: Winter in southern Arizona;
summer in northern Arizona
Habitat: Marshes, meadows

The Sora is a small, short-tailed, chicken-shaped rail with long, thin toes. Its plumage is mottled rusty brown above and grayish below with white barring along the belly and sides. The head has a black patch between the eye and bill, and the bill is yellow and conical. The tail is pointed and often cocked up and flicked. The juvenile is pale brown below with less black on the face. Soras feed along shorelines or at the edges of meadows for snails, insects, and aquatic plants. Their voice is a soft, rising *ooo-eep,* and they are quite tame, being seen more often than other rails. The breeding adult is illustrated.

Common Moorhen,

Gallinula chloropus
Family Rallidae (Rails, Coots)
Size: 14"
Season: Year-round
Habitat: Freshwater ponds and
wetlands

The Common Moorhen, like the American Coot, is actually a type of rail that behaves more like a duck. It paddles along, bobbing its head up and down, picking at the water surface for any small aquatic animals, insects, or plants. Having short wings, it is a poor flier, but its very long toes allow it to walk on floating vegetation. It is dark gray overall with a brownish back, black head, and white areas on the tail and sides. In breeding plumage the forehead shield is deep red, and the bill is red with a yellow tip. The breeding adult is illustrated.

American Coot,
Fulica americana
Family Rallidae (Rails, Coots)
Size: 15"
Season: Year-round
Habitat: Wetlands, ponds, urban lawns and parks

The American Coot has a plump body and a thick head and neck. It is a very common bird and becomes relatively tame in urban areas and parks. It dives for fish to feed, but it also dabbles like a duck or picks food from the ground. The coot is dark gray overall with a black head and white bill that ends with a dark narrow ring. The white trailing edge of the wings can be seen in flight. The toes are flanked with lobes that enable the coot to walk on water plants and swim efficiently. Juveniles are similar in plumage to adults but paler. Coots are often seen in very large flocks. The adult is illustrated.

Sandhill Crane, *Grus canadensis*
Family Gruidae (Cranes)
Size: 45"
Season: Winter
Habitat: Fields, shallow wetlands

The Sandhill Crane is a tall bird with long, strong legs, a long neck, and a long, straight bill. The long, thick tertial feathers create the distinctive bustle on the rear of all cranes. The top of the head is covered by bare red skin. Plumage is gray overall but may become spotted with rust-colored stains caused by preening with a bill stained by iron-rich mud. In flocks the cranes graze in fields, gleaning grains, insects, and small animals, and return to protected wetland areas in the evening to roost. The voice of the Sandhill Crane is a throaty, penetrating trumpeting sound. Unlike herons, cranes fly in groups with their necks extended. The adult is illustrated.

Killdeer, *Charadrius vociferus*
Family Charadriidae (Plovers)
Size: 10"
Season: Year-round
Habitat: Inland fields, farmlands, lakeshores, meadows

AVOCETS, STILTS

The Killdeer gets its name from its piercing *kill-dee* call, which is often heard before the well-camouflaged plover is seen. Well adapted to human-altered environments, it is quite widespread and gregarious. It has long, pointed wings, a long tail, and a conspicuous double-banded breast. The upper parts are dark brown, the belly is white, and the head is patterned with a white supercilium and forehead. The tail is rusty orange with a black tip. In flight there is a noticeable white stripe across the flight feathers. The Killdeer is known for the classic "broken wing" display that it uses to distract predators from its nest and young. The adult is illustrated.

American Avocet,
Recurvirostra americana
Family Recurvirostridae
(Avocets, Stilts)
Size: 18"
Season: Summer
Habitat: Shallow wetlands, marshes

The elegant American Avocet has a long, delicate, upturned black bill and long, thin blue-gray legs. The upperparts are patterned black and white, the belly is white, and the head and neck are light orange brown punctuated by black eyes. The bill of the female is slightly shorter than that of the male and has a greater bend. Nonbreeding adults have a pale gray head and neck. Avocets use a side-to-side sweeping motion of the bill to stir up small crustaceans and insect larvae as they wade methodically through the shallows. They may even submerge their heads as the water deepens. They are adept swimmers and emit a *wheet!* call in alarm. The breeding female (top) and breeding male (bottom) are illustrated.

Black-necked Stilt,
Himantopus mexicanus
Family Recurvirostridae (Avocets, Stilts)
Size: 14"
Season: Year-round
Habitat: Shallow wetlands,
marshes, lagoons

The Black-necked Stilt literally looks like a tiny body on stilts. It has extremely long, delicate red legs and a thin, straight, needle-like black bill. The wings and mantle are black, and the underparts and tail are white. The head is dark above with a white patch above the eye. The female has a slightly lighter, brownish back. In flight the long legs dangle behind the bird. To forage, it strides along to pick small prey from the water or vegetation, and it may voice a strident, barking *kek!* in alarm. Stilts are also known to perform the broken wing or broken leg act to distract predators. The adult male is illustrated.

Spotted Sandpiper, *Actitus macularius*
Family Scolopacidae (Sandpipers, Phalaropes)
Size: 7.5"
Season: Winter in southern Arizona,
summer in northern Arizona
Habitat: Streamsides, edges of lakes
and ponds

The solitary Spotted Sandpiper is known for its exaggerated, constant bobbing motion. It has a compact body, long tail, and short neck and legs. Plumage is brown above and light below with a white shoulder patch. There are a white eye ring and superciliary stripe above the dark eye line. In breeding plumage the sandpiper develops heavy spotting from chin to lower flanks and barring on the back. The bill is orange with a dark tip. The Spotted Sandpiper has short wings, and in flight the thin white stripe on the upper wing can be seen. To forage, it teeters about, picking small water prey and insects from the shoreline. The breeding adult is illustrated.

Greater Yellowlegs,
Tringa melanoleuca
Family Scolopacidae (Sandpipers, Phalaropes)
Size: 14"
Season: Winter in southern Arizona; spring and fall migration elsewhere
Habitat: Marshes

The Greater Yellowlegs is sometimes called the "tell-tale" bird, as the sentinel of a flock raises an alarm when danger is near, flying off and circling to return. It has long, bright yellow legs, a long neck, a dark, slightly upturned bill, and a white eye ring. The upperparts are dark gray and mottled, while the underparts are white with barring on the flanks. In breeding plumage the barring is noticeably darker and more extensive. To feed, the Greater Yellowlegs strides forward actively to pick small aquatic prey from the water or to chase fish. The Lesser Yellowlegs is similar but smaller. The nonbreeding adult is illustrated.

Western Sandpiper,
Calidris mauri
Family Scolopacidae (Sandpipers, Phalaropes)
Size: 6.5"
Season: Spring and fall migrant
Habitat: Wetlands, mudflats

The Western Sandpiper is one of the "peeps," or very small sandpipers. It has a relatively long black bill that droops slightly and black legs. In winter it is pale gray brown above and white below. In breeding plumage it has rufous on the scapulars and face and much darker streaking on the breast and back. A thin white stripe on the upper wing is visible in flight, along with a white rump with a dark central stripe. Western Sandpipers feed in shallow water or at the tide line, probing or picking invertebrates and insects. They often form rather large flocks. The nonbreeding adult (top) and breeding adult (bottom) are illustrated.

Wilson's Snipe, *Gallinago delicata*
Family Scolopacidae (Sandpipers, Phalaropes)
Size: 10.5"
Season: Winter
Habitat: Saltwater and freshwater marshes

Previously known as the Common Snipe (a Eurasian species), the Wilson's Snipe is a cryptically marked, short-necked shorebird with a long, straight bill. The head is striped, and the back is flanked with white stripes bordering the scapulars. The underside is white with extensive dark barring, and the legs are short and pale greenish yellow. Plumage is similar in all seasons. While feeding, the snipe probes rhythmically and deeply into the muddy substrate to extract worms, insect larvae, and crustaceans. It voices a loud *skipe!* when alarmed, or a *whit-whit-whit-whit*. Secretive and solitary, it abruptly lifts into flight when alarmed. Its flight is erratic and zigzagging and includes displays of "winnowing," where air across the tail feathers whistles during a steep descent. The adult is illustrated.

Wilson's Phalarope,
Phalaropus tricolor
Family Scolopacidae (Sandpipers, Phalaropes)
Size: 9"
Season: Spring and fall migrant
Habitat: Shallow pools around grassy or muddy wetlands

The Wilson's Phalarope is a small, thin, elegant shorebird with a relatively long neck and a long, needlelike black bill. With phalaropes, the female is the more brightly colored sex. In breeding plumage the female has a gray-brown back, clean white underparts, and a pale orange-brown foreneck. A thin black stripe runs from the bill, across the eye, and down the neck to the back. The head has pale cheeks and a gray crown, and the legs are black. Winter plumage is pale gray above and white below, and the legs are yellow. The breeding male looks like the winter adult female, with a dark eye stripe, crown, and nape. The Wilson's Phalarope actively walks along shorelines or swims in circles to find insects or plant material. Illustration shows breeding male (top) and breeding female (bottom).

Ring-billed Gull,

Larus delewarensis
Family Laridae (Gulls, Terns)
Size: 18"
Season: Winter
Habitat: Lakes, ponds

The Ring-billed Gull is common and quite tame. It is a relatively small gull with a rounded white head and a yellow bill with a dark subterminal ring. It has a pale gray back with black primaries tipped with white, and white underparts. The eyes are pale yellow, and the legs are yellow. The nonbreeding adult has faint streaking on the nape and around the eyes. Ring-billed Gulls feed on the water or on the ground, taking a wide variety of food, and may scavenge in urban areas and dumps. The nonbreeding adult is illustrated.

Bonaparte's Gull,

Chroicocephalus philadelphia
Family Laridae (Gulls, Terns)
Size: 13"
Season: Spring and fall migrant
Habitat: Lakes, wetlands

The Bonaparte's Gull is a small gull named after an American ornithologist who was related to Napoleon. It is agile and ternlike in flight, skimming low over the water to snatch fish. It has a thin, sharp black bill and red legs. Plumage in breeding season includes a black head that contrasts with its white body and light gray back and wings. The primaries form a white triangle against the dark trailing edge when the gull is in flight. The nonbreeding adult has a mostly white head with black eyes and small dark spots around the ears. A solitary gull, the Bonaparte does not form large flocks. It builds nests made of sticks in evergreen trees. The breeding adult (bottom) and nonbreeding adult (top) are illustrated.

California Gull,
Larus californicus
Family Laridae (Gulls, Terns)
Size: 21"
Season: Spring and fall migrant
Habitat: Lakes, rivers, prairie wetlands

The California Gull is a medium-size gull with a relatively thin, long bill. The breeding adult is medium blue gray above, with white edges to the tertials and secondaries, and is white below. The primaries are black with white spotting, and the tail is white. The head is rounded, the eyes are dark, and the bill is yellow orange with a black-and-red spot near the tip. The legs are greenish yellow. Winter adults show brownish streaking on the nape. California Gulls breed in large colonies and feed on a variety of food, including fish, small mammals, and insects. The gull's voice is a harsh squawk. The breeding adult is illustrated.

Black Tern, *Childonias niger*
Family Laridae (Gulls, Terns)
Size: 9.5"
Season: Spring and fall migrant
Habitat: Wet meadows, marshes, fields

The Black Tern is a small, dark tern with a very short, notched tail and a small, thin black bill. The breeding adult is dark gray above and black below with white undertail coverts and vent. The head is all black, and there is a hint of red at the gape. The tern's nonbreeding plumage is lighter gray above and all white below, with a white head except for black around the eye and at the rear of the crown. Black Terns fly low over the water or circle and hover, dropping down to capture insects, fish, and invertebrates. They do not plunge-dive like other terns. The breeding adult is illustrated.

Forster's Tern, *Sterna forsteri*
Family Laridae (Gulls, Terns)
Size: 14"
Season: Year-round
Habitat: Coastal areas, lakes, marshes

The Forster's Tern is a medium-size tern with no crest and a relatively long, pointed orange bill with a black tip. Breeding plumage is very pale gray above and white below with a forked white tail and very light primaries. The head has a black cap, and the short legs are red. Nonbreeding adults have darker primaries, a black ear patch in place of the cap, and an all-black bill. Forster's Terns display swallowlike flight, with narrow pointed wings, and they plunge-dive for fish. They voice short, harsh one-syllable calls. The nonbreeding adult (top) and breeding adult (bottom) are illustrated.

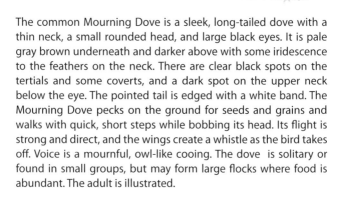

Mourning Dove, *Zenaida macroura*
Family Columbidae (Pigeons, Doves)
Size: 12"
Season: Year-round
Habitat: Open brushy areas, urban areas

The common Mourning Dove is a sleek, long-tailed dove with a thin neck, a small rounded head, and large black eyes. It is pale gray brown underneath and darker above with some iridescence to the feathers on the neck. There are clear black spots on the tertials and some coverts, and a dark spot on the upper neck below the eye. The pointed tail is edged with a white band. The Mourning Dove pecks on the ground for seeds and grains and walks with quick, short steps while bobbing its head. Its flight is strong and direct, and the wings create a whistle as the bird takes off. Voice is a mournful, owl-like cooing. The dove is solitary or found in small groups, but may form large flocks where food is abundant. The adult is illustrated.

Rock Dove, *Columba livia*
Family Columbidae (Pigeons, Doves)
Size: 12"
Season: Year-round
Habitat: Urban areas, farmland

The Rock Dove is the common pigeon seen in almost every urban area across the continent. Introduced from Europe, where they inhabit rocky cliffs, Rock Doves have adapted to city life, and domestication has resulted in a wide variety of plumage colors and patterns. The original wild version is a stocky gray bird with a darker head and neck and green to purple iridescence along the sides of the neck. The eyes are bright red, and the bill has a fleshy white cere on the base of the upper mandible. There are two dark bars across the back when the wing is folded. The rump is white, and the tail has a dark terminal band. Variants range from white to brown to black, with many pattern combinations. The adult is illustrated.

Band-tailed Pigeon,
Patagioenas fasciata
Family Columbidae (Pigeons, Doves)
Size: 14"
Season: Summer
Habitat: Mountainous pine woodlands, urban areas

The Band-tailed Pigeon is the largest pigeon and has a heavy body with a relatively long tail and a small, rounded head. Plumage is medium brownish gray overall with darker wings and a purplish brown cast to the breast. The bill is yellow with a black tip, the eye is dark with a red orbital ring, and the nape is iridescent green and bordered above by a thin, white band. The outer half of the tail has a broad, pale band. Band-tailed Pigeons consume a varied diet of insects, seeds, and berries, and voice a low, owl-like two-part *hoo-hoooo*. The adult is illustrated.

White-winged Dove,
Zenaida asiatica
Family Columbidae (Pigeons, Doves)
Size: 11.5"
Season: Year-round in southeastern Arizona; disperses north in summer
Habitat: Open woodlands, desert scrub, urban and agricultural areas

The White-winged Dove is similar in shape to the Mourning Dove but is heavier with a shorter tail and broader wings. It is brownish gray overall with dark wing tips and a broad white patch along the upper wing coverts that forms a white arc on the outer edges of the folded wing. The fanned tail shows white outer corners. There is a blue orbital ring around the brownish eye, and a black spot along the lower cheek. White-winged Doves forage for seeds, fruits, or cacti. The voice is an owl-like, mournful *whoo-whoo-ca-whoo*. Their range, once limited to far southern Texas, is expanding across the state as the bird adapts to most habitats, including urban areas. The adult is illustrated.

Inca Dove, *Columbina inca*
Family Columbidae (Pigeons, Doves)
Size: 8.25"
Season: Year-round
Habitat: Dry open woodlands, urban and agricultural areas

The Inca Dove is a small, squat terrestrial bird with a long tail and short legs. It is pale peachy gray overall with a distinctive scaled appearance due to the dark outer margins of its feathers. The outer tail feathers are white. The short, rounded wings are rufous brown tipped with black. This wing coloring is concealed in the folded wing but evident during flight or when the dove curiously lifts an extended wing skyward while on the ground. Juveniles are pale gray brown overall with no dark scaling. Inca Doves forage on the ground for seeds, and their call is a repetitive, two-part cooing. The adult is illustrated.

Yellow-billed Cuckoo,

Coccyzus americanus
Family Cuculidae (Cuckoos)
Size: 12"
Season: Summer
Habitat: Woodlands, streamsides, swamps

Like the other cuckoos, the Yellow-billed Cuckoo is secretive and shy, hiding in vegetation, where it picks insects, caterpillars, and fruit from trees. It is brown above with rufous flight feathers and crisp white below. The bill is yellow with black along the top ridge. The tail is long and graduated with large white spots on the underside. The cuckoo voices a quick, tapping *kak-kak-kak* or a series of throaty *coo* notes. The adult is illustrated.

Greater Roadrunner,

Geococcyx californianus
Family Cuculidae (Cuckoos)
Size: 23"
Season: Year-round
Habitat: Open fields, grasslands, urban areas

The Greater Roadrunner is a very large ground-dwelling cuckoo with rounded wings, a long tail, a long neck, and a strong, pointed bill. It is heavily streaked overall, except for its pale gray belly. A pale blue patch appears behind the eye, and its short, shaggy crest is often raised. The legs are long and sturdy. Roadrunners run with their tail held horizontal and their neck outstretched, and rarely fly. They forage by chasing down reptiles, insects, and rodents. Call is a deep cooing. The adult is illustrated.

Barn Owl, *Tyto alba*
Family Tytonidae (Barn Owl)
Size: 23"
Season: Year-round
Habitat: Barns, farmland, open areas with mature trees

The Barn Owl is a large-headed pale owl with small dark eyes, a heart-shaped facial disk, and long feathered legs. The wings, back, tail, and crown are light rusty brown with light gray smudging and small white dots. The underside, face, and underwing linings are white with spots of rust on the breast. Females are usually darker than males, with more color and spotting across the breast and sides. The facial disk is enclosed by a thin line of darker feathers. Barn Owls are nocturnal hunters for rodents, and their call is a haunting, raspy *screeee!* The adult male is illustrated.

Western Screech-Owl,
Megascops kennicottii
Family Strigidae (Typical Owls)
Size: 8.5"
Season: Year-round
Habitat: Wooded areas or parks; places where cavity-bearing trees exist

The Western Screech-Owl is a small, eared owl with a big head, short tail, and bright yellow eyes. The highly camouflaged plumage ranges from brown to gray, depending on the region. It is darker above, streaked and barred below. The ear tufts may be drawn back to give the appearance of a rounded head, and the bill is grayish green tipped with white. White spots on the margins of the coverts and scapulars create two white bars on the folded wing. The owl is a nocturnal bird, hunting during the night for small mammals, insects, or fish. Its voice is a descending, whistling call or a rapid staccato of one pitch. The adult is illustrated.

Great Horned Owl,
Bubo virginianus
Family Strigidae (Typical Owls)
Size: 22"
Season: Year-round
Habitat: Almost any environment, from forests to plains to urban areas

Found throughout North America, the Great Horned Owl is a large, strong owl with an obvious facial disk and long, sharp talons. Plumage is variable: Pacific and eastern forms are brown overall with heavy barring, a brown face, and a white chin patch, while southwestern forms are grayer and paler. The prominent ear tufts give the owl its name, and the eyes are large and yellow. The Great Horned Owl has exceptional hearing and sight. It feeds at night, perching on branches or posts and then swooping down on silent wings to catch birds, snakes, or mammals up to the size of a cat. Voice is a low *hoo-hoo-hoo*. The adult is illustrated.

Northern Pygmy-Owl,
Glaucidium gnoma
Family Strigidae (Typical Owls)
Size: 6.75"
Season: Year-round
Habitat: Mixed woodlands, wooded riparian areas

The Northern Pygmy-Owl is a tiny but tough owl with a compact, round body, bright yellow eyes, and a long tail. The upperparts and head are brown with white spotting; the tail is brown with white bars. The underparts are white with broad, dark brown streaks, while the flanks, sides, and breast are brown. There are white "eyebrows" continuing to the bill, and the throat is white (not often visible on the perched bird). This fierce bird hunts mostly during twilight hours for insects or vertebrates, sometimes taking prey as big as itself. The voice is a short, soft, repeated *hoot* from high in the trees; the owl may be lured into view by imitating its call. Its flight is undulating on short, rounded wings. The adult is illustrated.

Burrowing Owl,
Athene cunicularia
Family Strigidae (Typical Owls)
Size: 9.5"
Season: Year-round in southern Arizona; summer elsewhere
Habitat: Open grasslands and plains

The Burrowing Owl is a ground-dwelling owl that lives in burrows vacated by ground squirrels and other rodents. It is small and flat-headed and has a short tail and long legs. Plumage is brown spotted with white above and extensively barred brown and white below. The owl has a white chin and throat and bright yellow eyes. Burrowing Owls can be seen day or night perched on the ground or on a post, scanning for insects and small rodents. They sometimes exhibit a bowing movement when approached. Voice is a chattering or cooing, and sometimes imitative of a rattlesnake. The adult is illustrated.

Spotted Owl, *Strix occidentalis*
Family Strigidae (Typical Owls)
Size: 18"
Season: Year-round
Habitat: Old-growth woodlands

The Spotted Owl is a docile, medium-size, crestless owl with large black eyes and a short tail. The upperparts and head are dark brown with extensive white spotting, while the underside is whitish or light brown with dark brown barring (unlike the streaking of the similar Barred Owl). The bill is dull yellow, and the feet are mostly feathered. The voice is a throaty, booming, repeated *hoo-hoo-hoo* or a high-pitched, ascending squeak. These owls are nocturnal, hunting through the night for small mammals. Spotted Owls have declined in numbers because of the destruction of old-growth forests, upon which they rely for nesting cavities. The adult is illustrated.

Common Poorwill,
Phalaenoptilus nuttallii
Family Caprimulgidae
(Nightjars, Nighthawks)
Size: 8"
Season: Summer
Habitat: Arid plains and shrubland, rocky areas

The Common Poorwill is a very small nightjar with an oversize head, rounded wings, and a very short, stubby tail. Plumage is cryptically mottled and barred grayish overall with a white chin stripe and darker areas around the eye and upper breast. The outer edges of the tail are white, and the wings are brown with dark barring. The tiny bill is based with heavy whiskers. From a ground perch, Common Poorwills flutter up to catch insects in flight. They are mostly nocturnal and ground-dwelling, and may even hibernate during winter months. The adult is illustrated.

Common Nighthawk,
Chordeiles minor
Family Caprimulgidae (Nightjars, Nighthawks)
Size: 9"
Season: Summer
Habitat: Forests, marshes, plains, urban areas

The Common Nighthawk is primarily nocturnal, but may often be seen flying during the day and evening hours, catching insects on the wing with bounding flight. It is cryptically mottled gray, brown, and black with strong barring on an otherwise pale underside. In the male, a white breast band is evident. The tail is long and slightly notched, and the wings are long and pointed, extending past the tail in the perched bird. In flight there is a distinct white patch on both sides of the wings. During the day the Common Nighthawk is usually seen roosting on posts or branches with its eyes closed. Its voice is a short, nasal, buzzing sound. The adult male is illustrated.

White-throated Swift,

Aeronautes saxatalis
Family Apodidae (Swifts)
Size: 6"
Season: Year-round in southern Arizona; summer elsewhere
Habitat: Areas near cliffs, crevices, canyons

The White-throated Swift is a large, speedy swift with swooping, pointed wings and a slightly forked tail. It is black overall with crisp white patches along the belly, on the sides of the rump, and on the lower half of the head, extending above the eye. The wings of swifts are bent near the body, unlike swallows with the wings bent farther out. A highly aerial bird, the swift spends most of the day in flight, reaching incredible speeds using fast wing beats and gliding high in the air. It roosts in cracks and crevices during the night. The adult is illustrated.

Black-chinned Hummingbird,

Archilochus alexandri
Family Trochilidae (Hummingbirds)
Size: 3.5"
Season: Summer
Habitat: Riparian areas in woodlands, canyons, areas with oak trees

The Black-chinned Hummingbird is a small, delicate bird able to hover on wings that beat at a blinding speed. The long, needlelike bill is used to probe deep into flowers so that the bird can lap up nectar. The body is white below and green above, and the feet are tiny. Males have a dark green crown and an iridescent violet and black throat, or gorget. Females lack the colored gorget and have a light green crown and white-tipped tail feathers. Their behavior is typical of hummingbirds, hovering and buzzing from flower to flower, emitting chits and squeaks. Most of these birds migrate across the Gulf of Mexico to South America in the winter. The adult female (top) and male (bottom) are illustrated.

Anna's Hummingbird,
Calypte anna
Family Trochilidae (Hummingbirds)
Size: 4"
Season: Year-round in southern and western Arizona
Habitat: Woodlands, chaparral, streams, gardens

Anna's Hummingbird is a compact hummingbird with a long tail and a thin, straight, relatively short bill. The male has green upperparts, dark gray wings, and a pale underside with green barring. The cap and throat (gorget) are brilliant, iridescent rosy red, contrasting with a white eye ring. The female has a green crown and a pale throat with limited red feathers that sometimes form a central spot. Anna's Hummingbird hovers to sip nectar from flowers or feeders and sometimes eats small insects. Its voice is a series of scratchy, rattling cheeps and chips. Males are very territorial and exhibit dramatic display behavior by swooping down and into a steep upward arc. The adult male (bottom) and female (top) are illustrated.

Costa's Hummingbird,
Calypte costae
Family Trochilidae (Hummingbirds)
Size: 3.5"
Season: Year-round in southwestern Arizona; summer elsewhere
Habitat: Deserts, chaparral

Costa's Hummingbird is a tiny, plump-bellied hummingbird with a short tail and a relatively large head. Both sexes are green above and white below with pale green along the sides. The corners of the tail are black, tipped with white. The male has a brilliant, iridescent violet-blue crown and throat patch (gorget) that extends down the neck to a point. The female has a white head with a green crown and nape and a grayish auricular patch. Costa's Hummingbird drinks nectar from flowers or eats small insects. Its voice is a short, repeated *tic-tic* or a song of very high-pitched, airy, ascending then descending notes. The adult male (bottom) and female (top) are illustrated.

Rufous Hummingbird,
Selasphorus rufus
Family Trochilidae (Hummingbirds)
Size: 3.5"
Season: Spring and fall migrant
Habitat: Woodlands, parks, gardens

The Rufous Hummingbird is a small, compact hummingbird with a relatively short bill and short wings. The male is bright rufous orange with green wings, a white breast patch, and an iridescent bronze gorget (throat patch). The tail is tipped with black. The female has white tips on the outer tail feathers, a green back and crown, and a whitish chin with rufous spotting that sometimes forms a congealed spot in the middle. Rufous Hummingbirds drink nectar from flowers and feeders and sometimes eat small insects. The adult female (top) and male (bottom) are illustrated.

Elegant Trogon,
Trogon elegans
Family Trogonidae (Trogons)
Size: 12.5"
Season: Summer
Habitat: Streamsides in mountainous woodlands

The far southeastern corner of Arizona is the only reliable place in the United States to see the beautiful Elegant Trogon. It is a stocky, thick-necked bird with a stubby bill and a long, squared tail. The male is dark iridescent green above and on the head and breast, with gray wings. The underside is red orange with a white breast band. The tail is brown above and banded gray and white below. The female is much paler overall, gray brown above and mostly whitish below the breast with red at the lower belly. There is also a white patch behind the eye. Elegant Trogons forage in the tree canopy for insects and fruits, and voice a series of low, raspy notes. The adult female (top) and male (bottom) are illustrated.

Belted Kingfisher,
Megaceryle alcyon
Family Alcedinidae (Kingfishers)
Size: 13"
Season: Year-round in east-central
Arizona; winter elsewhere
Habitat: Creeks, lakes

The widespread but solitary Belted Kingfisher is a stocky, large-headed bird with a powerful, long bill and shaggy crest. It is grayish blue green above and white below with a thick blue band across the breast and white dotting on the back. White spots are at the lores. The female has an extra breast band of rufous and is rufous along the flanks. Belted Kingfishers feed by springing from a perch along the water's edge or by hovering above the water and then plunging headfirst to snatch fish, frogs, or tadpoles. Its flight is uneven, and its voice is a raspy, rattling sound. The adult female is illustrated.

Green Kingfisher,
Chloroceryle americana
Family Alcedinidae (Kingfishers)
Size: 8.75"
Season: Year-round
Habitat: Small streams,
lakesides with bushy shores

The Green Kingfisher is a very small kingfisher with a relatively large head and a massive, daggerlike bill. It is emerald green above and on the head, with white spotting on the wings and tail and a broad, white collar about the neck. It is white below with a rufous breast band (male) or double green breast bands (female). The forehead and top of the head are flat and meet with a crest on the hind crown. Green Kingfishers plunge-dive for small fish and amphibians from a perch or after coursing low over the water surface. The voice is a curious, two-part tapping sound, similar to rocks clinking together. Green Kingfishers are quieter and more secretive than the larger Belted Kingfishers, and they often twitch or pump their tails. The adult male is illustrated.

Lewis's Woodpecker,
Melanerpes lewis
Family Picidae (Woodpeckers)
Size: 11"
Season: Year-round
Habitat: Open woodlands, streamsides

Lewis's Woodpecker is large and mostly dark. Plumage is greenish black above and gray below, fading to a dusky rose color on the belly. The gray of the breast continues around the neck to form a light collar. The head is dark; deep red in front surrounded by greenish-black plumage. The long, stiff tail feathers support the bird while it is perched on vertical trunks. In flight Lewis's Woodpeckers are steady and direct, not undulating like most woodpeckers. From a perch on the tree trunk, they fly out to catch insects or eat nuts they have stored in cavities. They are often seen in groups. The adult is illustrated.

Acorn Woodpecker,
Melanerpes formicivorus
Family Picidae (Woodpeckers)
Size: 9"
Season: Year-round
Habitat: Oak woodlands

The comical Acorn Woodpecker is a loud and social woodpecker that inhabits large oak trees in large, busy colonies. The back, wings and tail are glossy black, and the rump and base of the primaries are white. Below, it has a black breast bib that dissolves in thin streaks to a white belly. The distinctively patterned head is black at and behind the eye, whitish or very pale yellow on the forehead and chin, and red on the hind crown. Females have a black patch on the crown. Acorn Woodpeckers eat mostly acorns, which they store tightly packed in holes they have drilled out. Their voice consists of chattering and loud squawks, as well as drumming sounds. The adult male is illustrated.

Gila Woodpecker,

Melanerpes uropygialis
Family Picidae (Woodpeckers)
Size: 9"
Season: Year-round
Habitat: Desert scrub,
arid woodlands

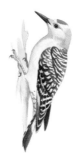

The Gila Woodpecker is a conspicuous, medium-size woodpecker with a long neck and bill. The upperparts and wings are barred black and white, and the underparts and head are pale sandy brown. The belly is washed with yellow and has dark bars that continue to the undertail coverts. The male has a red crown that is absent in the female and juvenile. Gila Woodpeckers feed in trees and cacti, or on the ground for insects, reptiles, and fruits; they may also visit rural feeders. The voice is a long series of high-pitched *yip-yip-yip* notes, sung from a conspicuous perch atop a cactus; drumming is also common. The adult male is illustrated.

Red-naped Sapsucker,

Sphyrapicus nuchalis
Family Picidae (Woodpeckers)
Size: 8.5"
Season: Year-round
Habitat: Woodlands, suburbs, areas
with standing dead trees

The sapsuckers are named for their habit of drilling rows of pits in tree bark, then returning to eat the sap that emerges and the insects that come to investigate. They also flycatch and eat berries. The Red-naped Sapsucker is medium-size with pied black-and-white plumage and barring across the back. The head is boldly patterned in black and white with a red crown and red chin (white in females). The belly is unbarred and pale yellow, while the flanks are white with black barring. In flight there is a distinct white patch on the upper wing. This bird was once considered the same species as the eastern Yellow-bellied Sapsucker. The adult male is illustrated.

Arizona Woodpecker,
Picoides arizonae
Family Picidae (Woodpeckers)
Size: 7.5"
Season: Year-round
Habitat: Mixed oak woodlands of southeast Arizona

Formerly known as Strickland's Woodpecker, the Arizona Woodpecker is a small but large-headed woodpecker, and the only one with a brown back. The upperparts are dark brown with white spotting on the flight feathers and outer tail feathers. The underside is white and heavily spotted and barred with brown. The face and chin are white with dark brown markings along the malar area, behind the eye, and across the top of the head. The male and juvenile have a red patch across the back of the crown. Arizona Woodpeckers peck away bark to find insects and voice repeated, high-pitched, raspy squeaks and squawks. The adult male is illustrated.

Downy Woodpecker,
Picoides pubescens
Family Picidae (Woodpeckers)
Size: 6.5"
Season: Year-round
Habitat: Woodlands, parks in urban areas, streamsides

The Downy Woodpecker is a tiny woodpecker with a small bill and a relatively large head. It is white underneath with no barring, has black wings barred with white, and has a patch of white on the back. The head is boldly patterned black and white, and the male sports a red nape patch. The base of the bill joins the head with fluffy nasal tufts. Juveniles may show some red on the forehead and crown. Downy Woodpeckers forage for berries and insects in the bark and among the smaller twigs of trees. The very similar Hairy Woodpecker is larger with a longer bill and more aggressive foraging behavior, sticking to larger branches and not clinging to twigs. The adult male is illustrated.

Northern Flicker,

Colaptes auratus
Family Picidae (Woodpeckers)
Size: 12.5"
Season: Year-round
Habitat: Variety of habitats,
including suburbs and parks

The common Northern Flicker is a large, long-tailed woodpecker often seen foraging on the ground for ants and other small insects. It is barred brown and black across the back, and buff with black spotting below. The head is brown with a gray nape and crown. On the upper breast is a prominent half-circle of black, and the male has a red patch at the malar region. Flight is undulating and shows an orange wing lining and white rump. The flicker's voice is a loud, sharp *keee,* and it sometimes drums its bill repeatedly at objects, like a jackhammer. The Northern Flicker is sometimes referred to as the Red-shafted Flicker and is very similar to the Gilded Flicker. The adult male is illustrated.

WOODPECKERS

PASSERINES

Olive-sided Flycatcher,

Contopus cooperi
Family Tyrannidae (Tyrant Flycatchers)
Size: 7.5"
Season: Summer
Habitat: Open coniferous woodlands

The Olive-sided Flycatcher is a stocky flycatcher with a relatively large head, a thick neck, and a short, slightly notched tail. It is dark olive gray above, on the head, and on the sides, with a white strip that runs down the middle of the belly and up to the chin, forming a sort of "vest" shape. The sides of the rump are white, but this is usually concealed in the perched bird. The bill is stout, thick at the base, and pointed. The Olive-sided Flycatcher perches on high, bare treetop branches and flycatches for insects. Its voice is a high-pitched *whip wee weer,* sometimes dubbed *quick three beers*. The adult is illustrated.

Western Wood-Pewee,

Contopus sordidulus
Family Tyrannidae (Tyrant Flycatchers)
Size: 6.25"
Season: Summer
Habitat: Woodland edges, canyons, creek sides

The Western Wood-Pewee is a large-headed, thick-necked flycatcher with drab plumage overall. It is brownish gray or olive gray with pale whitish or dusky underparts and gray sides that meet at the breast. A very slight eye ring surrounds the dark eye, and the bill is thin, pointed, and has a pale lower mandible. There are thin wing bars along the coverts and edges of the tertials. This pewee is nearly identical to the Eastern Wood-Pewee, but the ranges do not normally overlap. Western Wood-Pewees flycatch for insects, starting from a high perch and then returning to the same spot. The voice is composed of shrill, high-pitched *pee-wee* notes. The adult is illustrated.

Willow Flycatcher,
Empidonax traillii
Family Tyrannidae (Tyrant Flycatchers)
Size: 5.75"
Season: Summer
Habitat: Moist, brushy areas with willows; foothill fields

The Willow Flycatcher is similar to many flycatchers in the genus *Empidonax*. It has a crown that peaks at the rear of the head and a fairly thick bill. Plumage is greenish brown gray above with pale, dusky underparts and a whitish chin and throat. A thin white eye ring encircles the eye, the lores are light, and the lower mandible is pale orange. Distinct wing bars are visible on the folded wing. Willow Flycatchers catch insects, starting from a perch and then returning to the same spot. Their voice is a high, nasal *fitz-bee* call. The adult is illustrated.

Black Phoebe, *Sayornis nigricans*
Family Tyrannidae (Tyrant Flycatchers)
Size: 7"
Season: Year-round
Habitat: Open woodlands, gardens, shrubs—usually near water

The Black Phoebe is a long-tailed flycatcher with a relatively big head and a short, thin, pointed bill. Plumage is sooty black above, on the head, and on the breast and sides. It is white underneath, coming to a point at the breast. The crown is often peaked, and the outer tail feathers show a thin white stripe. Black Phoebes perch upright and bob their tails up and down, and they voice a high-pitched, whistled *seep*. They flycatch for insects from a low perch and are often seen hovering. The adult is illustrated.

Say's Phoebe,

Sayornis saya
Family Tyrannidae (Tyrant Flycatchers)
Size: 7.5"
Season: Year-round
Habitat: Arid open country, shrubland

Say's Phoebe is a fairly slim flycatcher with a long black tail. It is pale gray brown above with lighter wing bars. The underside is whitish to gray under the chin and breast, fading to orange brown on the belly and undertail coverts. The head has a flat crown that often peaks toward the rear, and the bird has dark eyes, lores, and bill. It flycatches for insects from a perch on rocks or twigs. Say's Phoebe voices a high, whistled *pit-eur* and often pumps or flares out its tail. The adult is illustrated.

Vermilion Flycatcher,

Pyrocephalus rubinus
Family Tyrannidae (Tyrant Flycatchers)
Size: 6"
Season: Year-round in southern Arizona
Habitat: Open brushlands or woodlands, usually near water

The unmistakable Vermilion Flycatcher is a small but large-headed flycatcher with a short, thin bill. The sexes are dramatically different in plumage. Males are dark gray brown on the back, tail, and wings, and vermilion red below and on the head. A dark stripe runs through the eye, and the red crown is often raised. The female is pale brown above and white below with gray streaking on the breast and a pinkish-buff wash on the lower belly and undertail coverts. The face is white with a brown auricular patch and crown. Vermilion Flycatchers spring from a low perch to flycatch for insects, and voice a high-pitched, accelerating series of quick chips, ending in a short trill. The male (left) and female (right) are illustrated.

Western Kingbird,
Tyrannus verticalis
Family Tyrannidae (Tyrant Flycatchers)
Size: 8.75"
Season: Summer
Habitat: Open fields, agricultural areas

The Western Kingbird is a relatively slender flycatcher with a stout black bill and a slightly rounded black tail with white along the outer edge. It is grayish or greenish brown above, pale gray on the breast, and bright yellow on the belly, sides, and undertail coverts. The head is light gray with a white throat and malar area, and dark gray at the lores and behind the eye. A small, reddish crown patch is normally concealed. The Western Kingbird flycatches for insects from a perch on a branch, post, or wire, and its voice is composed of quick, high-pitched zips and chits. The adult is illustrated.

Loggerhead Shrike,
Lanius ludovicianus
Family Laniidae (Shrikes)
Size: 9.5"
Season: Year-round
Habitat: Dry open country

The solitary Loggerhead Shrike is raptorlike in its feeding habits. It swoops down from its perch on a branch, wire, or post and captures large insects, small mammals, or birds, impaling them on thorny barbs before tearing them apart to feed. It is a compact, large-headed bird with a short, thick, slightly hooked bill. The upperparts are gray, and the underparts are pale. The wings are black with white patches at the base of the primaries and upper coverts. The tail is black and edged with white. A black mask on the head extends from the base of the bill to the ear area. Juveniles show a finely barred breast. Flight is composed of quick wing beats and swooping glides. The adult is illustrated.

Warbling Vireo, *Vireo gilvus*
Family Vireonidae (Vireos)
Size: 5.5"
Season: Summer
Habitat: Moist deciduous woodlands;
parks

The Warbling Vireo is a plain, light-colored, stocky vireo with a fairly short hooked bill. The upperparts are pale brownish or greenish gray with no distinct wing bars, and the underside is whitish or washed with pale yellow brown. The dark eyes contrast with the light superciliary stripes and lores. The underside of the wing is two-toned with light linings and darker flight feathers. Warbling Vireos forage in trees for insects and berries and sing a high-pitched, warbling song. The adult is illustrated.

Steller's Jay,
Cyanocitta stelleri
Family Corvidae (Jays, Crows)
Size: 11.5"
Season: Year-round
Habitat: Coniferous forests,
mountainous areas

Steller's Jay is a bold, stocky, crested jay with short, broad wings. The tail, back, wings, and belly are bright deep blue, while the mantle and breast are sooty gray. The black head has a thick, pointed crest, and inland races have white eyebrows and thin white streaks on the forehead. The legs and bill are stout and strong. Steller's Jays eat a wide variety of food, from nuts, insects, and berries to picnic scraps. Their voice is a loud, raucous squawking, and they sometimes mimic the calls of other birds. The adult is illustrated.

Pinyon Jay,
Gymnorhinus cyanocephalus
Family Corvidae (Jays, Crows)
Size: 10.5"
Season: Year-round
Habitat: Juniper-pinyon scrub, open pine forests

The Pinyon Jay is a highly social, plain-colored, crestless jay with a short, squarish tail and a thin, pointed bill. Plumage is pale gray blue overall, and even paler underneath. The head is a brighter blue with dark lores, and the throat is streaked with pale gray. Pinyon Jays favor the nuts from the pinyon pine, as well as berries and other seeds. They voice a nasal, loud *caw-caw-caw*. They form huge feeding flocks and breeding colonies. Their flight is direct, without undulations. The adult is illustrated.

Western Scrub-Jay,
Aphelocoma californica
Family Corvidae (Jays, Crows)
Size: 11.5"
Season: Year-round
Habitat: Open scrub-oak, urban areas

The Western Scrub-Jay is a long-necked, sleek, crestless jay. The upperparts are deep blue with a distinct, lighter gray-brown mantle. The underparts are pale gray, becoming white on the belly and undertail coverts. The jay has a thin white superciliary stripe and a dark gray malar area. The throat is streaked with white and gray above a pale, gray-blue "necklace" across the breast. Flight is an undulating combination of rapid wing beats and swooping glides. The jay's diet consists of nuts, seeds, insects, and fruit. The adult is illustrated.

Clark's Nutcracker,
Nucifraga columbiana
Family Corvidae (Jays, Crows)
Size: 12"
Season: Year-round
Habitat: Coniferous forests of high
mountain areas

Clark's Nutcracker is a chunky, wily, crestless jay with long wings and a stout, thick-based bill. Plumage is gray or brownish gray overall with black wings and a two-toned, black-and-white tail. There is a prominent white patch on the outer secondary feathers. The head has deep black eyes surrounded by whitish areas and a black bill. The nutcrackers forage in trees and along the ground for pine nuts, insects, and fruit, but also scavenge at picnic grounds. Clark's Nutcrackers walk with a swaying, crowlike gait and voice loud, harsh, rattling squawks. The adult is illustrated.

American Crow,
Corvus brachyrhynchos
Family Corvidae (Jays, Crows)
Size: 17.5"
Season: Year-round
Habitat: Open woodlands, pastures,
rural fields, dumps

The American Crow is a widespread corvid found across the continent, voicing its familiar, loud, grating *caw-caw*. It is a large, stocky bird with a short, rounded tail, broad wings, and a thick, powerful bill. Plumage is glistening black overall in all stages of development. The crow eats almost anything and often forms loose flocks with other crows. The adult is illustrated.

Black-billed Magpie,
Pica hudsonia
Family Corvidae (Jays, Crows)
Size: 19"
Season: Year-round
Habitat: Riparian areas,
open woodlands, pastures, rural areas
of northern Arizona

The Black-billed Magpie is a heavy, broad-winged bird with an extremely long, graduated tail. It has striking pied plumage: black on the head, upper breast, and back; dark, iridescent green blue on the wings and tail; and crisp white on the scapulars and belly. The legs are dark and stout, and the bill is thick at the base. Juvenile birds have a much shorter tail. Magpies travel in small groups and are opportunistic feeders of insects, nuts, eggs, and carrion. The voice is a whining, questioning *mag?* or a harsh *wok-wok*. The adult is illustrated.

Common Raven, *Corvus corax*
Family Corvidae (Jays, Crows)
Size: 24"
Season: Year-round
Habitat: Deserts, mountains, canyons, forests

The Common Raven is a stocky, gruff, large corvid with a long, massive bill that slopes directly into the forehead. The wings are narrow and long, and the tail is rounded or wedge-shaped. The entire body is glossy black, sometimes bluish, and the neck is laced with pointed, shaggy feathers. Quite omnivorous, the raven feeds on carrion, refuse, insects, and roadkill, and has a varied voice that includes deep croaking. Ravens may soar and engage in rather acrobatic flight. Crows are similar but smaller, with proportionally smaller bills. The adult is illustrated.

Horned Lark, *Eremophila alpestris*
Family Alaudidae (Larks)
Size: 7"
Season: Year-round
Habitat: Open and barren country

The Horned Lark is a slim, elongated, ground-dwelling bird with long wings. The plumage is pale reddish gray above and whitish below with variable amounts of rusty smudging or streaking on the breast and sides. The head is boldly patterned with a black crown, cheek patch, and breast bar, contrasting with a yellow throat and white face. In females the black markings are much paler. Particularly evident on males are feather tufts, or "horns," on the sides of the crown. Outer tail feathers are black. Horned Larks scurry on the ground, foraging for plant matter and insects, and sing with rapid, musical warbles and chips. The adult male is illustrated.

SWALLOWS

Purple Martin, *Progne subis*
Family Hirundinidae (Swallows)
Size: 8"
Season: Summer
Habitat: Marshes, open water, agricultural areas

The Purple Martin is the largest North American swallow. It has long, pointed wings, a streamlined body, and a forked tail. The bill is very short and broad at the base. The male is dark overall with a blackish-blue sheen across the back and head, while the female is paler overall with sooty, mottled underparts. Flight consists of fast wing beats alternating with circular glides. Purple Martins commonly use man-made nest boxes or tree hollows as nesting sites. The adult male is illustrated.

Northern Rough-winged
Swallow, *Stelgidopteryx serripennis*
Family Hirundinidae (Swallows)
Size: 5.5"
Season: Year-round
Habitat: Sandy cliffs, steep stream-
sides, outcrops, bridges

The Northern Rough-winged Swallow flies in a smooth and even fashion with full wing beats, feeding on insects caught on the wing. It is uniform brownish above and white below. The breast is lightly streaked with pale brown, and the tail is short and square. Juveniles show light rust-colored wing bars on the upper coverts. These fairly solitary swallows find nesting sites in holes in sandy cliffs. The adult is illustrated.

Tree Swallow, *Tachycineta bicolor*
Family Hirundinidae (Swallows)
Size: 5.75"
Season: Year-round
Habitat: Variety of habitats near water
and perching sites

The Tree Swallow has a short, slightly notched tail, broad-based triangular wings, and a thick neck. It has a high-contrast plumage pattern with dark, metallic green-blue upperparts and crisp white underparts. When perched, the primaries reach just past the tail tip. Juveniles are gray brown below with a subtle, darker breast band. Tree Swallows take insects on the wing, but also eat berries and fruits. They often form huge lines of individuals perched on wires or branches. Voice is a high-pitched chirping. The adult male is illustrated.

Violet-green Swallow,
Tachycineta Thalassina
Family Hirundinidae (Swallows)
Size: 5.25"
Season: Year-round
Habitat: Forested areas, especially near water and cliffs

The Violet-green Swallow is a slim, boldly patterned swallow with long wings and a short, notched tail. The wings and tail are dark brown black, the back is glossy green, and the uppertail coverts and wing coverts are dark purplish. The swallow is pure white underneath; the white coloring extends to the sides of the rump and up to the face. The top of the head is green. Females are paler and brownish on the back with gray smudging on the face. Violet-green Swallows are highly aerial and catch small insects on the wing, but often settle on a perch in plain view. The call includes thin, high-pitched tweets and cheeps. The adult male is illustrated.

Mountain Chickadee,
Poecile gambeli
Family Paridae (Chickadees, Titmice)
Size: 5.25"
Season: Year-round
Habitat: Mountainous woodlands

The Mountain Chickadee is a small, fluffy bird with a tiny bill, similar to the Black-capped Chickadee, but with a white superciliary stripe through the black cap. It is grayish above with pale gray or buff-colored underparts, and has a black crown and chin patch. Energetic and acrobatic, it travels in small groups eating small insects and seeds gleaned from tree branches. Its voice sounds like *chick-a-dee-dee-dee*. The adult is illustrated.

Bridled Titmouse,
Baeolophus wollweberi
Family Paridae (Chickadees, Titmice)
Size: 5.25"
Season: Year-round
Habitat: Higher-elevation oak woodlands,
riparian areas

The Bridled Titmouse is a tiny but large-headed songbird with a short bill and high crest. It is gray above and on the tail; paler gray below. The head is white with black "bridled" markings on the face with a tall, pointed gray crest. The Bridled Titmouse flits acrobatically among the foliage to glean insects, and voices a series of high, whistled notes like *peka-peeka-peeka* or dry, chirping notes. It is common in Mexico but reaches its northernmost range in southern Arizona and New Mexico. The adult is illustrated.

Verdin, *Auriparus flaviceps*
Family Remizidae (Verdins)
Size: 4.5"
Season: Year-round
Habitat: Low-elevation desert
scrublands

The Verdin is a solitary, small bird with a small, sharp bill and chickadee-like habits. It is gray overall, paler below, with a golden-yellow head and a small, rufous shoulder patch. Sexes are similar, but the females have less yellow on the head and are duller overall. Juveniles are entirely gray. Verdins actively flit among thorny thickets, foraging for insects. The voice is a clear, high-pitched, whistled *tew*. The adult male is illustrated.

Bushtit, *Psaltriparus minimus*
Family Aegithalidae (Bushtit)
Size: 4.5"
Season: Year-round
Habitat: Mixed woodlands,
scrubland, oaks

The Bushtit is a tiny, ball-shaped, fluffy bird with short, rounded wings and a long tail. Its drab plumage is brownish gray above and paler gray underneath. The eye of the female is light yellow, while that of the male is black. The bill is short and stubby with a curved culmen, and the legs are thin and dark. Bushtits flit from tree to tree in noisy groups, eating berries and insects. Voice is a thin, high-pitched, rapid series of twittering chips. The adult female is illustrated.

NUTHATCHES

White-breasted Nuthatch,
Sitta carolinensis
Family Sittidae (Nuthatches)
Size: 5.75"
Season: Year-round
Habitat: Mixed oak and coniferous
woodlands

The White-breasted Nuthatch has a large head and wide neck, short rounded wings, and a short tail. It is blue gray above and pale gray below with rusty smudging on the lower flanks and undertail coverts. The breast and face are white, and there is a black crown merging with the mantle. The bill is long, thin, and upturned at the tip. To forage, the nuthatch creeps headfirst down tree trunks to pick out insects and seeds. It nests in tree cavities high off the ground. Voice is a nasal, repetitive *auk-auk-auk*. The adult male is illustrated.

Red-breasted Nuthatch,
Sitta canadensis
Family Sittidae (Nuthatches)
Size: 4.5"
Season: Year-round
Habitat: Open coniferous and
oak forests

The Red-breasted Nuthatch is a small, stubby, large-headed, short-tailed bird with a long, thin, slightly upturned bill. Plumage is blue gray above and rusty orange or buff (in the female) below. The head is white with a black crown and eye stripe. The nuthatch's legs are short, but its toes are very long to aid in grasping tree bark. Nuthatches creep downward headfirst on tree trunks and branches to pick out insects and seeds. The call is a nasal, repetitive *yonk, yonk, yonk*. The adult male is illustrated.

Brown Creeper,
Certhia americana
Family Certhiidae (Creepers)
Size: 5.25"
Season: Year-round
Habitat: Mature woodlands

The Brown Creeper is a small, cryptically colored bird with a long, pointed tail and a long, down-curved bill. It is mottled black, brown, and white above and plain white below, fading to brownish toward the rear. The face has a pale supercilium and a white chin. The legs are short with long, grasping toes. Brown Creepers spiral upward on tree trunks, probing for insects in the bark, then fly to the bottom of another tree to repeat the process. Its stiff tail aids in propping the bird up, like a woodpecker's tail. Its voice is composed of thin, high-pitched *seet* notes. The adult is illustrated.

CREEPERS

Rock Wren, *Salpinctes obsoletus*
Family Troglodytidae (Wrens)
Size: 6"
Season: Year-round
Habitat: Open, dry, rocky areas
and deserts

The Rock Wren is a stocky bird with a short tail, a large head, and a thin, slightly downcurved bill. It is grayish brown above with fine barring and spotting. Underneath it is pale buff to gray with fine streaking along the breast and dark bars on the undertail coverts. There is a pale superciliary stripe above the dark eye. The pale brownish tips of the outer tail feathers can be seen when the tail is fanned. Rock Wrens search around rocks for insects, flitting from rock to rock and often bobbing up and down. The adult is illustrated.

Canyon Wren,
Catherpes mexicanus
Family Troglodytidae (Wrens)
Size: 5.75"
Season: Year-round
Habitat: Rocky cliffs and canyons,
rocky streamsides

The Canyon Wren has a short tail, a flat head, and a long, slightly downcurved bill. It is rufous brown with black barring and spotting on the back, tail, and underparts. The head is gray brown above and white below the eyes, with a white throat and breast. Juveniles are patterned as adults but lack spotting on the back and belly. Canyon Wrens deftly scramble among rocks, reaching into tight crevices to pick out insects and spiders. The voice is a series of sweet, musical notes followed by dry, buzzy notes. The adult is illustrated.

Cactus Wren,
Campylorhynchus brunneicapillus
Family Troglodytidae (Wrens)
Size: 8.5"
Season: Year-round
Habitat: Low-elevation desert scrub

WRENS

The Cactus Wren is the state bird of Arizona and is structurally like a small, plump thrasher with a long bill and a slightly curved upper culmen. It is brownish above and on the tail, both heavily mottled with white and black. The underside is whitish, becoming buff toward the vent, and spotted with black dots that coalesce at the breast. The head has a chocolate-brown crown above a broad, white supercilium. Cactus Wrens forage mostly on the ground, picking and scraping for insects and seeds. The voice is a series of short, raucous notes, increasing in volume, often sung from a perch atop a cactus with the tail lowered. The adult is illustrated.

Marsh Wren, *Cistothorus palustris*
Family Troglodytidae (Wrens)
Size: 5"
Season: Winter
Habitat: Marshes, reeds, stream banks

The Marsh Wren is a small, cryptic, rufous-brown wren with a normally cocked-up tail. The tail and wings are barred with black, and the chin and breast are white. There is a well-defined white superciliary stripe below a uniform brown crown, and the mantle shows distinct black-and-white striping. The bill is long and slightly decurved. Marsh Wrens are vocal day and night with quick, repetitive cheeping. They are secretive but inquisitive, and glean insects from the marsh vegetation and water surface. The adult is illustrated.

Blue-gray Gnatcatcher,

Polioptila caerulea
Family Polioptilidae (Gnatcatchers)
Size: 4.5"
Season: Year-round
Habitat: Deciduous or pine woodlands, thickets

The Blue-gray Gnatcatcher is a tiny, energetic, long-tailed bird with a narrow, pointed bill and thin dark legs. It is blue-gray above and pale gray below, with white edges to the tertials creating a light patch on the middle of the folded wing. The tail is rounded and has black inner and white outer feathers. The eye is surrounded by a crisp white eye ring. Males are brighter blue overall and have a darker supraloral line than females. To forage, gnatcatchers flit through thickets and catch insects in the air. They often twitch and fan their tails. Voice is a high-pitched buzzing or cheeping sound, sometimes sounding like the calls of other birds. The adult male is illustrated.

American Dipper,

Cinclus mexicanus
Family Cinclidae (Dippers)
Size: 7.5"
Season: Year-round
Habitat: Fast-flowing, rocky, mountainous streams

The American Dipper is an unusual, plump, aquatic songbird with a short tail, long legs, and a short, thin bill. The plumage is dense and usually disheveled, slate gray overall with a brownish hue on the head. Thin white crescents are sometimes visible around the dark eyes. Dippers perch on rocks in a stream and plunge into the water, propelled by their wings, to pick out larvae and insects. Sometimes they use their long toes to cling to underwater rocks. They fly low above the water surface, and course up and down stream corridors. While perched, they constantly bob their bodies up and down. The dipper is also known as the Water Ouzel. The adult is illustrated.

DIPPERS

Golden-crowned Kinglet

Regulus satrapa
Family Regulidae (Kinglets)
Size: 4"
Season: Year-round
Habitat: Mixed woodlands,
brushy areas

The Golden-crowned Kinglet is a tiny, plump songbird with a short tail and a short, pointed bill. It is greenish gray above and pale gray below, with wings patterned in black, white, and green. The face has a dark eye stripe and crown, and the center of the crown is golden yellow and sometimes raised. The legs are dark with orange toes. Kinglets are in constant motion, flitting and dangling among branches, sometimes hanging upside down or hovering at the edges of branches to feed. Their voice includes very high-pitched *tzee* notes. The adult is illustrated.

Ruby-crowned Kinglet,

Regulus calendula
Family Regulidae (Kinglets)
Size: 4"
Season: Winter
Habitat: Mixed woodlands,
brushy areas

The Ruby-crowned Kinglet is a tiny, plump songbird with a short tail and a diminutive, thin bill. It has a habit of nervously twitching its wings as it actively flits through vegetation, gleaning small insects and larvae. It may also hover in search of food. Plumage is pale olive green above and paler below, with patterned wings and pale wing bars on the upper coverts. There are white eye rings or crescents around the eyes. The bright red crest of the male bird is faintly noticeable unless the crest is raised. Voice is a very high-pitched, whistling *seeee*. The adult male is illustrated.

Western Bluebird,
Sialia mexicana
Family Turdidae (Thrushes)
Size: 7"
Season: Year-round
Habitat: Open woodlands, pastures, fields

The Western Bluebird travels in small groups, feeding on a variety of insects, spiders, and berries. It is stocky, short-tailed, and short-billed, and often perches with an upright posture on wires and posts. The male is brilliant blue above and rusty orange below with a blue belly and undertail region. The orange extends to the nape, making a subtle collar. The female is paler overall with a pale throat and eye ring. Juveniles are brownish gray with extensive white spotting and barred underparts. Man-made nest boxes have helped this species increase in numbers throughout its range. The male (bottom) and female (top) are illustrated.

Mountain Bluebird,
Sialia currucoides
Family Turdidae (Thrushes)
Size: 7.25"
Season: Year-round in northeastern Arizona; winter elsewhere
Habitat: Open mountain meadows, sage land

Compared to other bluebirds, the Mountain Bluebird has a thinner bill, a longer tail, and longer wings. The male is bright sky blue overall, somewhat paler below, and nearly white at the undertail coverts. The female retains the blue color on the tail and wings, but is pale gray on the back, underparts, and head, with a noticeable white eye ring. Juveniles are similar to females, but darker on the back and spotted below. From perches on branches or posts, Mountain Bluebirds dart out to catch insects. They form large winter flocks and tend to hold their bodies in a horizontal posture. The adult male is illustrated.

Townsend's Solitaire,
Myadestes townsendi
Family Turdidae (Thrushes)
Size: 8.5"
Season: Year-round in northeastern Arizona; disperses in winter
Habitat: Mountainous coniferous woodlands, juniper scrub

Townsend's Solitaire is a slim, elongated thrush with a short, blunt bill. It often perches upright on bare branches with its long tail drooping down. It is grayish overall, darker on the wings and tail, with buff-colored patches at the base of the flight feathers. The eyes are dark with distinctive white eye rings. White outer tail feathers are evident on the fanned tail. The juvenile is darker with extensive light spotting. Townsend's Solitaires forage for insects, seeds, and pine nuts. The adult is illustrated.

American Robin,
Turdus migratorius
Family Turdidae (Thrushes)
Size: 10"
Season: Year-round
Habitat: Widespread in a variety of habitats, including woodlands, fields, parks, lawns

Familiar and friendly, the American Robin is a large thrush with a long tail and long legs. It commonly holds its head cocked and keeps its wing tips lowered beneath its tail. It is gray brown above and rufous below with a darker head and contrasting white eye crescents and loral patches. The chin is streaked black and white, and the bill is yellow with darker edges. Females are typically paler overall than males, and juveniles show white spots above and dark spots below. Robins forage on the ground, picking out earthworms and insects, or in trees for berries. Song is a series of high, musical phrases, sounding like *cheery, cheer-u-up, cheerio*. The adult male is illustrated.

Hermit Thrush,

Catharus guttatus
Family Turdidae (Thrushes)
Size: 7"
Season: Year-round
Habitat: Woodlands, brushy areas

The Hermit Thrush is a compact, short-tailed thrush that habitually cocks its tail. It forages on the ground near vegetative cover for insects, worms, and berries, and voices a song of beautiful, flutelike notes. It is reddish to olive brown above with a rufous tail. The underparts are white with dusky flanks and sides and black spotting on the throat and breast. The dark eyes are encircled by complete white eye rings. In flight the pale wing lining contrasts with the dark flight feathers. The adult is illustrated.

Northern Mockingbird,

Mimus polyglottos
Family Mimidae (Mockingbirds, Catbirds, Thrashers)
Size: 10.5"
Season: Year-round
Habitat: Open fields, grassy areas near vegetative cover, suburbs, parks

The Northern Mockingbird is constantly vocalizing. Its scientific name, *polyglottos,* means "many voices," alluding to its amazing mimicry of the songs of other birds. It is sleek, long-tailed, and long-legged. Plumage is gray above, with darker wings and tail, and off-white to brownish gray below. It has two white wing bars, a short, dark eye stripe, and a pale eye ring. In flight conspicuous white patches on the inner primaries and coverts and white outer tail feathers can be seen. Like other mimids, the mockingbird forages on the ground for insects and berries, intermittently flicking its wings. The adult is illustrated.

Brown Thrasher,

Toxostoma rufum
Family Mimidae (Mockingbirds,
Catbirds, Thrashers)
Size: 11"
Season: Year-round in eastern Texas;
winter elsewhere
Habitat: Woodlands, thickets, urban gardens, orchards

The Brown Thrasher is primarily a ground-dwelling bird that thrashes through leaves and dirt for insects and plant material. It has a long tail and legs with a medium-length, slightly decurved bill. Plumage is rufous brown above, including the tail, and whitish below, heavily streaked with brown or black. There are two prominent pale wing bars and pale outermost corners to the tail. The eyes are yellow to orange. The thrasher's voice is a variety of musical phrases, often sung from a conspicuous perch. The adult is illustrated.

Curve-billed Thrasher,

Toxostoma curvirostre
Family Mimidae (Mockingbirds, Catbirds, Thrashers)
Size: 11"
Season: Year-round
Habitat: Dry brushlands, deserts, urban areas

The Curve-billed Thrasher is a stocky, long-tailed, long-legged bird with a long, downcurved bill. It is gray brown overall, paler below, with faint white wing bars and brownish spotting down the breast and belly. The eyes are bright orange, and the corners of the tail are white. The thrasher forages on the ground, probing the substrate and flicking away debris to find insects, seeds, and berries. The voice is a whistling *wit-weet* and a series of rapid, rambling, musical notes. The adult is illustrated.

Sage Thrasher,
Oreoscoptes montanus
Family Mimidae (Mockingbirds, Catbirds, Thrashers)
Size: 8.5"
Season: Year-round
Habitat: Dry brushlands, deserts, urban areas

The Sage Thrasher is a relatively small thrasher with a long tail and wings and a shorter, slightly curved bill. It is brownish gray above, with thin, white bars on the wing coverts. The underside is white or pale buff, with extensive dark streaking. The eyes are bright yellow, and there are white corners to the otherwise dark brown tail. Sage Thrashers run or fly low above the ground when foraging for insects, and they vocalize a variety of melodious warbles, sometimes mimicking other birds. The adult is illustrated.

European Starling,
Sturnus vulgaris
Family Sturnidae (Starlings)
Size: 8.5"
Season: Year-round
Habitat: Almost anywhere, particularly in rural fields, gardens, dumps, urban parks

Introduced from Europe, the European Starling has successfully infiltrated most habitats in North America and competes with native birds for nest cavities. It is a stocky, sturdy, aggressive bird that is glossy black overall with a sheen of green or purple. The breeding adult has a yellow bill and greater iridescence, while the adult in winter is more flat black with a black bill and numerous white spots. The tail is short and square. Starlings form very large, compact flocks and fly directly on pointed, triangular wings. The diet of starlings is highly variable and includes insects, grains, and berries. Vocalizations include loud, wheezy whistles and clucks and imitations of other birdsongs. The breeding adult is illustrated.

American Pipit,
Anthus rubescens
Family Motacillidae (Pipits)
Size: 6.5"
Season: Winter
Habitat: Fields of short grass,
lake shorelines

The American Pipit is a slim, ground-dwelling, sparrow-size bird with long legs and a thin, pointed bill. It is grayish brown above and buff or whitish underneath, with pale wing bars and variable amounts of dark streaking down the breast, sides, and flanks. The head is gray brown with a lighter supercilium and malar area. There are white outer tail feathers on an otherwise dark tail. Pipits walk upright in small groups while foraging for insects on the ground, and often pump and wag their tails. The adult is illustrated.

Cedar Waxwing,
Bombycilla cedrorum
Family Bombycillidae (Waxwings)
Size: 7"
Season: Winter
Habitat: Woodlands, swamps,
urban areas near berry trees

The Cedar Waxwing is a compact, crested songbird with pointed wings and a short tail. The sleek, smooth plumage is brownish gray overall with paler underparts, a yellowish wash on the belly, and white undertail coverts. The head pattern is striking with a crisp black mask thinly bordered by white. The tail is tipped with bright yellow, and the tips of the secondary feathers are coated with a unique, red waxy substance. Cedar Waxwings form large flocks and devour berries from a tree, then move on to the next. They may also flycatch small insects. Voice is an extremely high-pitched, whistling *seee*. The adult is illustrated.

Phainopepla,
Phainopepla nitens
Family Ptilogonatidae (Silky-Flycatchers)
Size: 7.75"
Season: Year-round
Habitat: Desert scrub, dry open woodlands of southern
and western Arizona

The Phainopepla is a slim, sleek bird resembling a flycatcher with
a tall, shaggy crest and a long, rounded tail. The male is uniformly
glossy black overall with a white wing patch that is only visible in
flight. The female is gray overall with white margins to the wing
feathers and pale underwing coverts. Both sexes have red eyes
and short bills. Phainopeplas feed on insects and berries, favoring
mistletoe. Among their many voices are a series of nasal, gurgling
notes, a high-pitched warble, and mimicked songs of other birds.
They often perch in plain view, and their flight is jerky and flutter-
ing. The adult male is illustrated.

Orange-crowned Warbler,
Oreothlypis celata
Family Parulidae (Wood-Warblers)
Size: 5"
Season: Year-round
Habitat: Mixed woodlands,
brushy thickets

The Orange-crowned Warbler is rather plain with a relatively long
tail and a thin, pointed bill. It is olive green above and brighter
yellow below, streaked with olive. The undertail coverts are solid
yellow. The warbler has a short, dark eye line and a thin, pale, broken eye ring. There is much variation in this species, from brighter
forms to grayer forms, and the orange crown patch is rarely visible. Orange-crowned Warblers forage for insects or berries in the
undergrowth, and voice a long series of descending staccato *tit*
notes. The adult is illustrated.

Lucy's Warbler,
Oreothlypis luciae
Family Parulidae (Wood-Warblers)
Size: 4.25"
Season: Summer
Habitat: Mesquite brush, arid mixed woodlands near water

Lucy's Warbler is a tiny, plain-colored, desert-dwelling warbler with a thin bill. The upperparts and head are pale gray with a rufous rump patch, while the underparts are whitish with a very pale, buff wash. White lores and eye rings encompass the dark eyes, and males exhibit a spotty, reddish crown patch. Lucy's Warblers actively flit through foliage for insects and often pump their tails. The voice is a series of short, high *sit* notes and melodious cheeping. The adult male is illustrated.

Yellow Warbler,
Setophaga petechia
Family Parulidae (Wood-Warblers)
Size: 5"
Season: Summer
Habitat: Willows and alders near streamsides, rural shrubbery, gardens

The Yellow Warbler is widespread in North America and sings a musical *sweet-sweet-sweet*. It is bright yellow overall with darker yellow green above and reddish-brown streaking below. The black eyes stand out on its light face, and the bill is relatively thick for a warbler. Clean yellow stripes are evident on the fanned tail. The female is paler overall with less noticeable streaking on the breast and sides. Yellow Warblers forage in the brush for insects and spiders. The adult male is illustrated.

Yellow-rumped Warbler,
Setophaga coronata
Family Parulidae (Wood-Warblers)
Size: 5.5"
Season: Year-round
Habitat: Deciduous and coniferous woodlands, suburbs

Two races of this species occur in North America: The "myrtle" form ranges across the continent, and the "Audubon's" form can be found west of the Rockies and throughout Arizona. The "myrtle" variety is blue gray above with dark streaks, and white below with black streaking below the chin and a bright yellow side patch. There is a black mask across the face, bordered by a thin superciliary stripe above and a white throat below. The nonbreeding adult and female are paler, with a more brownish cast to the upperparts. The longish tail has white spots on either side and meets with the conspicuous yellow rump. The "Audubon's" variety has a yellow chin and a gray face. Yellow-rumped Warblers prefer to eat berries and insects. The adult male "myrtle" form is illustrated.

Black-throated Gray Warbler,
Setophaga nigrescens
Family Parulidae (Wood-Warblers)
Size: 5.5"
Season: Summer
Habitat: Oak and pinyon-juniper woodlands, dry pine foothills

The Black-throated Gray Warbler is a boldly patterned, black-and-white warbler with a relatively thick, pointed bill. It is slate gray above, streaked on the mantle, with clear white wing bars. Underneath it is white, streaked with black that merges into a black throat, and the outer tail feathers are white. The head has white patches below and above the eyes, and there are yellow loral patches. The female has less barring underneath than the male and a black throat. The warblers actively forage through foliage for insects and voice a series of wheezy notes, ascending in volume, sounding like *wee-wee-wee-wee-weet*. The adult male is illustrated.

American Redstart,

Setophaga ruticilla
Family Parulidae (Wood-Warblers)
Size: 5"
Season: Spring and fall migrant
Habitat: Open mixed woodlands in early succession

The constantly active, frenetic American Redstart often fans its tail and wings in display while perched. It is long-tailed, and the plumages of males and females are markedly different. The male is jet black above and white below with a fiery red patch at the side of its breast and a paler, peachy-red color in a wing bar and on the sides of its tail. The female is gray green above with a slate-gray head and white chin and breast. The colored areas are located on the same parts as on the male, but are yellow. Redstarts eat insects gleaned from branches and bark, or flycatch for insects. The adult male (bottom) and female (top) are illustrated.

Macgillivray's Warbler,

Geothlypis tolmiei
Family Parulidae (Wood-Warblers)
Size: 5.25"
Season: Summer
Habitat: Woodlands with dense undergrowth, riparian areas

MacGillivray's Warbler is similar to its eastern counterpart, the Mourning Warbler, but has a slightly longer tail and more prominent white eye arcs. Plumage is olive green above and on the tail, and yellow below, with darker sides and flanks. The head and breast are slate gray; slightly paler in females. The warblers feed on insects, hopping and flitting through the vegetation, sometimes pumping their tails. The adult male is illustrated.

WOOD-WARBLERS

Common Yellowthroat,

Geothlypis trichas
Family Parulidae (Wood-Warblers)
Size: 5"
Season: Summer
Habitat: Low vegetation near water,
swamps, fields

The Common Yellowthroat scampers through the undergrowth looking for insects and spiders in a somewhat wrenlike manner. It is a plump little warbler that often cocks up its tail. Plumage is olive brown above and pale brown to whitish below, with a bright yellow breast/chin region and undertail coverts. The male has a black facial mask trailed by a fuzzy white area on the nape. The female lacks the facial mask. The adult female (top) and male (bottom) are illustrated.

Wilson's Warbler,

Cardellina pusilla
Family Parulidae (Wood-Warblers)
Size: 4.75"
Season: Spring and fall migrant
Habitat: Willow and alder thickets,
woodlands near water

Wilson's Warbler is a small, lively warbler with a narrow tail and a short bill. It is uniformly olive green above and yellow below with some olive-green smudging. The head has large black eyes and a beanie-shaped black cap. Females and juveniles have a greenish cap with variable amounts of black. Wilson's Warblers stay low to the ground, gleaning food from the vegetation, or hover and fly-catch for insects. Their voice is a rapid series of chattering notes or a quick *chip* call. The adult male is illustrated.

Green-tailed Towhee,
Pipilo chlorurus
Family Emberizidae (Sparrows, Buntings)
Size: 7.25"
Season: Winter in southern Arizona; summer elsewhere
Habitat: Dense scrub of higher elevations

The Green-tailed Towhee is a secretive, small towhee with a long tail and a short, conical bill. It is gray overall with yellow green on the wings, back, and tail. On the head is a rufous crown (often held erect), white throat, white malar stripe, and white supraloral patch. Sexes are similar, while the juvenile is heavily streaked with brown overall. Green-tailed Towhees scrape on the ground with both feet at once like other towhees, for seeds and insects. Their voice is a harsh, high, mewing squawk, a low, muffled *wok*, or a high sing-song melody. The adult is illustrated.

Spotted Towhee,
Pipilo maculatus
Family Emberizidae (Sparrows, Buntings)
Size: 8.5"
Season: Year-round
Habitat: Thickets, suburban shrubs, gardens

The Spotted Towhee is a large, long-tailed sparrow with a thick, short bill and sturdy legs. It forages on the ground in dense cover by kicking back both feet at once to uncover insects, seeds, and worms. It is black above, including the head and upper breast, and has rufous sides and a white belly. It has white wing bars, white spotting on the scapulars and mantle, and white corners on the tail. The eye color is red. Females look like the males but are brown above. The Spotted Towhee and the Eastern Towhee were previously considered one species, the Rufous-sided Towhee. The adult male is illustrated.

Chipping Sparrow,

Spizella passerina
Family Emberizidae (Sparrows, Buntings)
Size: 5.5"
Season: Year-round
Habitat: Dry fields, woodland edges, gardens

The Chipping Sparrow is a medium-size sparrow with a slightly notched tail and a rounded crest. It is barred black and brown on the upperparts, with a gray rump, and is pale gray below. The head has a rufous crown, white superciliary stripes, dark eye line, and white throat. The bill is short, conical, and pointed. The sexes are similar, and winter adults are duller and lack the rufous color on the crown. Chipping Sparrows feed in trees or on open ground in loose flocks, searching for seeds and insects. Voice is a rapid, staccato chipping sound. The breeding adult is illustrated.

Lark Sparrow,

Chondestes grammacus
Family Emberizidae (Sparrows, Buntings)
Size: 6.5"
Season: Winter in southern Arizona; summer in central and northern Arizona
Habitat: Woodland edges, dry prairies with brush, agricultural areas

The Lark Sparrow is an elongated, thin sparrow with a long, rounded tail. It is light brown above, streaked with dark brown, and white below with tan around the sides and flanks. There is a distinct dark spot in the middle of the breast. The head is patterned with a rufous crown that has a white medial stripe, rufous cheeks, black eye line, and black throat stripe. Lark Sparrows travel in small flocks, hopping or walking on the ground to pick up seeds and insects. They sing a variety of high-pitched chips and trills, often from a conspicuous perch. Males may display with their tails cocked up. The adult is illustrated.

SPARROWS, BUNTINGS

Lark Bunting,

Calamospiza melanocorys
Family Emberizidae (Sparrows, Buntings)
Size: 7"
Season: Winter in southern Arizona
Habitat: Open barren grasslands,
arid scrub, sage land

The Lark Bunting is a stocky, distinctive sparrow with a large head, a thick conical bill, a short notched tail, and short wings. It undergoes a dramatic change in plumage during the year. The breeding male is black overall with a large white patch on the wing coverts. The tail is tipped with white. The nonbreeding male and the female are brownish above with a pale underside that is extensively streaked with brown. The head is patterned with a white malar patch above a black throat stripe. The Lark Bunting forages on the ground for seeds and insects. The breeding male (bottom) and nonbreeding male (top) are illustrated.

White-crowned Sparrow,

Zonotrichia leucophrys
Family Emberizidae (Sparrows,
Buntings)
Size: 7"
Season: Winter
Habitat: Brushy areas, woodland
edges, gardens

The White-crowned Sparrow has a rounded head, sometimes with a raised peak, and a fairly long, slightly notched tail. It is brownish above, streaked on the mantle, and shows pale wing bars. The underside is grayish on the breast, fading to pale brown on the belly and flanks. The head is gray below the eye and boldly patterned black and white above the eye, with a white medial crown stripe. The bill is bright yellow orange. White-crowned Sparrows forage on the ground, often in loose flocks, scratching for insects, seeds, and berries. Their song is variable, but it usually starts with one longer whistle followed by several faster notes. The adult is illustrated.

Song Sparrow,
Melospiza melodia
Family Emberizidae (Sparrows, Buntings)
Size: 6"
Season: Year-round
Habitat: Thickets, shrubs, woodland edges near water

One of the most common sparrows, the Song Sparrow is fairly plump and has a long, rounded tail. It is brown and gray above with streaking, and white below with heavy dark or brownish streaking that often congeals into a discreet spot in the middle of the breast. The head has a dark crown with a gray medial stripe, dark eye line, and dark malar stripe above the white chin. Song Sparrows are usually seen in small groups or individually, foraging on the ground for insects and seeds. The song is a series of chips and trills of variable pitch, and the call is a *chip-chip-chip*. The adult is illustrated.

Dark-eyed Junco,
Junco hyemalis
Family Emberizidae (Sparrows, Buntings)
Size: 6"
Season: Year-round in northern Arizona; winter elsewhere
Habitat: Thickets, rural gardens, open coniferous or mixed woodlands

The Dark-eyed Junco is a small, plump sparrow with a short, conical, pink bill and several distinct variations in plumage. One of the more common races is the "Oregon" Junco, with a rusty brown mantle, sides, and flanks; a white belly; and a black head and breast. Sexes are similar, but the female is paler overall. The white outer tail feathers are obvious in flight. Juncos hop about on the ground, often in groups, picking up insects and seeds. Their voice is a staccato, monotone, chirping trill. Also common in Arizona is the Gray-headed Junco, which is pale gray overall with a rufous mantle. The adult male of the "Oregon" race is illustrated.

Summer Tanager,
Piranga rubra
Family Cardinalidae
(Tanagers, Grosbeaks)
Size: 7.75"
Season: Summer
Habitat: Mixed pine and oak woodlands

The Summer Tanager lives high in the tree canopy, where it voices a musical song and forages for insects and fruit. It is a relatively large, heavy-billed tanager with a crown that is often peaked in the middle. The male is variable shades of red over the entire body, while the female is olive or brownish yellow above and dull yellow below. Juveniles are similar to the females but have a patchy red head and breast. The adult male is illustrated.

Western Tanager,
Piranga ludoviciana
Family Cardinalidae
(Tanagers, Grosbeaks)
Size: 7.25"
Season: Summer
Habitat: Mixed or coniferous woodlands

The Western Tanager is a highly arboreal, brightly colored tanager with pointed wings and a short but thick bill. The breeding male has a black upper back, tail, and wings with a yellow shoulder patch and a white wing bar. The underside and rump are bright yellow, extending across the neck and nape, and the head is red orange. Females and winter males are paler with little or no red on the head. Western Tanagers forage for insects, primarily in the upper canopy of mature trees. They are usually difficult to see clearly, but their vocalizations of three-syllable, rattling high notes with changing accents are distinctive. The breeding male is illustrated.

TANAGERS, GROSBEAKS

Northern Cardinal,
Cardinalis cardinalis
Family Cardinalidae
(Tanagers, Grosbeaks)
Size: 8.5"
Season: Year-round
Habitat: Woodlands with thickets,
suburban gardens

The Northern Cardinal with its thick, powerful bill eats mostly seeds but also forages for fruit and insects. It is often found in pairs and is quite common at suburban feeders. It is a long-tailed songbird with a thick, short, orange bill and a tall crest. The male is red overall with a black mask and chin. The female is brownish above, dusky below, and crested, with a dark front to the face. Juveniles are similar to the female but have a black bill. The voice is a musical *weeta-weeta* or *woit,* heard from a tall, exposed perch. The adult male (bottom) and female (top) are illustrated.

Pyrrhuloxia, *Cardinalis sinuatus*
Family Cardinalidae
(Tanagers, Grosbeaks)
Size: 8.75"
Season: Year-round
Habitat: Desert scrub, arid open
woodlands

The Pyrrhuloxia is built like the Northern Cardinal with a long tail, a long pointed crest, and a short, thick yellow bill that is sharply curved. It is gray overall with patches of red on the tail, wings, crest, face, and in a stripe from the chin to the vent. The female is browner overall without red on the underparts and face. Pyrrhuloxias forage for insects and seeds. The voice is a series of a few high *wheet* notes, often sung while flicking the tail and erecting the crest. The adult male is illustrated.

Black-headed Grosbeak,

Pheucticus melanocephalus
Family Cardinalidae (Tanagers, Grosbeaks)
Size: 8.25"
Season: Summer in western Texas;
transient migrant elsewhere
Habitat: Open woodlands, gardens, riparian areas

The Black-headed Grosbeak is a chunky, large-headed, short-tailed songbird with a massive, thick-based bill that enables it to eat very large seeds. The breeding male is black on the mantle, wings, and tail with extensive white markings and streaks. The underparts, neck, and rump are rusty orange with whitish undertail coverts. The head is black, and the bill is pale on the lower mandible and dark on the upper. The female is brownish above and pale tan below with darker streaking. The head is brown with a white supercilium and malar patch. Black-headed Grosbeaks eat insects, fruits, and seeds and sometimes visit feeders. Their song consists of erratic, whistling warbles. The breeding female (top) and breeding male (bottom) are illustrated.

Blue Grosbeak, *Passerina caerulea*

Family Cardinalidae (Tanagers, Grosbeaks)
Size: 6.5"
Season: Summer
Habitat: Woodland edges, thickets, fields

The name "grosbeak" derives from the French word *gros,* meaning large, and refers to the birds' massive, conical bills. The male Blue Grosbeak is azure blue overall with rufous wing bars and shoulder patches. It is black at the front of the face and has a horn-colored bill. The female is brown overall and paler below with lighter wing bars and lores. The similar Indigo Bunting is smaller in size and smaller-billed and lacks the rufous color on the wings. Blue Grosbeaks eat seeds, fruit, and insects in open areas and habitually flick their tails. They often perch and sing a meandering, warbling song for extended periods. The female (top) and male (bottom) are illustrated.

Indigo Bunting, *Passerina cyanea*
Family Cardinalidae (Tanagers, Grosbeaks)
Size: 5.5"
Season: Summer
Habitat: Brush lands, open woodlands, fields

Often occurring in large flocks, the Indigo Bunting forages mostly on the ground for insects, berries, and seeds. It is a small, compact songbird with a short, thick bill. The male is entirely blue; the head is a dark purplish blue, and the body is a lighter, sky blue. The female is brownish gray above and duller below with faint streaking on the breast meeting a white throat. The winter male is smudged with patchy gray, brown, and white. Indigo Buntings perch in treetops voicing their undulating, chirping melodies. The breeding male (bottom) and female (top) are illustrated.

Western Meadowlark,
Sturnella neglecta
Family Icteridae (Blackbirds, Orioles, Grackles)
Size: 9.5"
Season: Year-round
Habitat: Open fields, grasslands, meadows

The Western Meadowlark is a chunky, short-tailed icterid with a flat head and a long, pointed bill. It is heavily streaked and barred above, and yellow beneath with dark streaking. The head has a dark crown, white superciliary stripes, dark eye lines, and a yellow chin and malar area. A black, V-shaped necklace that becomes quite pale during winter months is on the upper breast. Nonbreeding plumage is much paler overall. Meadowlarks gather in loose flocks to pick through grasses for insects and seeds. They often perch on telephone wires or posts to sing their short, whistling phrases. The breeding adult is illustrated.

Brown-headed Cowbird,
Molothrus ater
Family Icteridae (Blackbirds, Orioles, Grackles)
Size: 7.5"
Season: Year-round
Habitat: Woodland edges, pastures with livestock, grassy fields

The Brown-headed Cowbird is a stocky, short-winged, short-tailed blackbird with a short, conical bill. The male is glossy black overall with a chocolate-brown head, but is sometimes much lighter in western populations. The female is light brown overall with faint streaking on the underparts and a pale throat. Cowbirds often feed in flocks with other blackbirds, picking seeds and insects from the ground. Their voice is a number of gurgling, squeaking phrases. Cowbirds practice brood parasitism, whereby they lay their eggs in the nests of other passerine species that then raise their young. Hence, their presence often reduces the populations of other songbirds. The dark adult male is illustrated.

Yellow-headed Blackbird,
Xanthocephalus xanthocephalus
Family Icteridae (Blackbirds, Orioles, Grackles)
Size: 9.5", male larger than female
Season: Summer in northern Arizona; winter in southern Arizona
Habitat: Farmland, marshy areas with reeds or cattails

The Yellow-headed Blackbird is a large, bold blackbird with a relatively short tail and a deep-based, pointed, triangular bill. The male is black with a bright golden-yellow head and breast. The eyes and lores are black, and there is a white patch on the primary coverts. The female is dark brown with brown infusing the otherwise yellow head and white streaking that trickles from the yellow breast. The blackbird's song is a series of raucous, rattling, choking noises, often sung while the bird is perched and fluffing out its feathers. The female (top) and male (bottom) are illustrated.

Red-winged Blackbird,
Agelaius phoeniceus
Family Icteridae (Blackbirds, Orioles, Grackles)
Size: 8.5"
Season: Year-round
Habitat: Marshes, meadows, agricultural areas near water

The Red-winged Blackbird is a widespread, ubiquitous, chunky meadow-dweller that forms huge flocks during the nonbreeding season. The male is deep black overall with bright orange-red lesser coverts and pale medial coverts that form an obvious shoulder patch in flight but may be partially concealed on the perched bird. The female is barred tan and dark brown overall with a pale superciliary stripe and malar patch. Red-winged Blackbirds forage marshland for insects, spiders, and seeds. Voice is a loud, raspy, vibrating *konk-a-leee* given from a perch atop a tall reed or branch. The female (top) and male (bottom) are illustrated.

Brewer's Blackbird,
Euphagus cyanocephalus
Family Icteridae (Blackbirds, Orioles, Grackles)
Size: 9"
Season: Year-round
Habitat: Meadows, pastures, open woodlands, urban areas

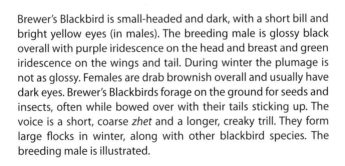

Brewer's Blackbird is small-headed and dark, with a short bill and bright yellow eyes (in males). The breeding male is glossy black overall with purple iridescence on the head and breast and green iridescence on the wings and tail. During winter the plumage is not as glossy. Females are drab brownish overall and usually have dark eyes. Brewer's Blackbirds forage on the ground for seeds and insects, often while bowed over with their tails sticking up. The voice is a short, coarse *zhet* and a longer, creaky trill. They form large flocks in winter, along with other blackbird species. The breeding male is illustrated.

Bullock's Oriole, *Icterus bullockii*
Family Icteridae (Blackbirds, Orioles, Grackles)
Size: 9"
Season: Summer
Habitat: Deciduous woodlands,
suburban gardens, parks

BLACKBIRDS, ORIOLES, GRACKLES

Bullock's Oriole is a flat-crowned and relatively short-tailed icterid with a pointed but broad-based bill. The male is black on the mantle and wings with a large white patch on the wing coverts and white edges to the flight feathers. The body and rump are golden orange, and the head is golden orange with a black chin, eye line, and crown. The tail is orange with a dark center and tips. Females are gray on the back, pale below, and yellow on the tail, head, and breast. Bullock's Orioles eat insects or berries in the tree canopy and sing in a series of chatterings and chips. Bullock's Oriole and the Baltimore Oriole are sometimes considered one species, the Northern Oriole. The breeding female (top) and breeding male (bottom) are illustrated.

Scott's Oriole, *Icterus parisorum*
Family Icteridae (Blackbirds, Orioles, Grackles)
Size: 9"
Season: Summer
Habitat: Arid open woodlands, often where yucca is present

Scott's Oriole is a medium-size oriole with a relatively long, sharply pointed bill. The male has black wings, back, breast, and an entirely black head. It is brilliant lemon yellow on the shoulder, rump, and underparts below the breast. The tail is black with yellow toward the base. Females are duller overall with a grayish-green head and tail and variable amounts of dark smudging on the breast and throat. Scott's Orioles forage through oaks, junipers, and yuccas for insects and nectar, and sing a series of sweet, melodious, whistled notes. The adult male (bottom) and female (top) are illustrated.

Evening Grosbeak,

Coccothraustes vespertinus
Family Fringillidae (Finches)
Size: 8"
Season: Year-round in eastern Arizona; winter to the west
Habitat: Coniferous or mixed woodlands, rural gardens

The Evening Grosbeak is a comical-looking finch with a large head, a short stubby tail, and an enormous conical bill. In the male, plumage fades from dark brown on the head to bright yellow toward the rump and belly. The wings are black with large white patches on the secondaries and tertials. The yellow superciliums merge with the flat forehead and meet the pale yellow-green bill. The legs are short and pinkish. Females are grayish overall with choppy white markings on the wings. Evening Grosbeaks travel in flocks to feed on seeds and berries in the upper canopy and often visit feeders, preferring sunflower seeds. The voice is a series of short, spaced, rattling *cheep* notes. The adult male (bottom) and female (top) are illustrated.

House Finch,

Carpodacus mexicanus
Family Fringillidae (Finches)
Size: 6"
Season: Year-round
Habitat: Woodland edges, urban areas

The House Finch is a western species that has been introduced to eastern North America and is now common and widespread across the country. It is a relatively slim finch with a longish, slightly notched tail and a short, conical bill with a down-curved culmen. The male is brown above, with streaking on the back, and pale below, with heavy streaking. An orange-red wash pervades the supercilium, throat, and upper breast. The female is a drab gray brown with similar streaking on the back and underside and no red on the face or breast. House Finches have a varied diet that includes seeds, insects, and fruit, and they are often the most abundant birds at feeders. Voice is a rapid, musical warble. The adult male is illustrated.

Pine Siskin, *Spinus pinus*
Family Fringillidae (Finches)
Size: 5"
Season: Year-round
Habitat: Coniferous woodlands, rural gardens

The Pine Siskin is a small, cryptically colored finch with a short tail and a narrow, pointed bill. The head and back are light brown overall, heavily streaked with darker brown. The underside is whitish and streaked in darker shades. There is a prominent yellow wing bar on the greater coverts, and yellow on the flight feather edges and at the base of the primaries. Females are marked similarly with a darker underside and white, not yellow, wing bars. Individuals can be quite variable as to the amount of streaking and the prominence of the yellow coloring. Pine Siskins forage energetically in small groups for seeds and insects, sometime clinging upside down on twigs to reach food. Their voice consists of high-pitched, erratic, raspy chips and trills. The adult male is illustrated.

American Goldfinch, *Spinus tristis*
Family Fringillidae (Finches)
Size: 5"
Season: Winter
Habitat: Open fields, marshes, urban feeders

The American Goldfinch is a small, cheerful, social finch with a short, notched tail and a small, conical bill. In winter it is brownish gray, lighter underneath, with black wings and tail. There are two white wing bars, and bright yellow on the shoulders, around the eyes, and along the chin. In breeding plumage the male becomes light yellow across the back, underside, and head; develops a black forehead and loreal area; and sees its bill turn orange. Females look similar to winter males. American Goldfinches forage by actively searching for insects and seeds of all kinds, particularly thistle seeds. Voice is a meandering, musical warble that includes high *cheep* notes. The breeding female (top) and breeding male (bottom) are illustrated.

House Sparrow,

Passer domesticus
Family Passeridae (Old World Sparrows)
Size: 6.25"
Season: Year-round
Habitat: Urban environments,
rural pastures

Introduced from Europe, the House Sparrow is ubiquitous in almost every city in the United States and is often the only sparrow-type bird seen in urban areas. It is stocky, aggressive, and gregarious, and has a relatively large head and a short, finch-like bill. Males are streaked brown and black above and are pale below. The lores, chin, and breast are black, while the crown and auriculars are gray. There are prominent white wing bars at the median coverts. In winter the male lacks the dark breast patch. Females are drab overall with a lighter bill and a pale supercilium. House Sparrows have a highly varied diet, including grains, insects, berries, and crumbs from the local cafe. Voice is a series of rather unmusical chirps. The breeding female (top) and breeding male (bottom) are illustrated.

Index

About the Author/Illustrator

Todd Telander is a naturalist/
illustrator/artist living in Walla
Walla, Washington. He has
studied and illustrated wildlife
since 1989, while living in California, Colorado, New Mexico,
and Washington. He graduated
from the University of California
at Santa Cruz with degrees in
biology, environmental studies,
and scientific illustration and
has since illustrated numerous
books and other publications,

including FalconGuides' Scats and Tracks series. His wife, Kirsten
Telander, is a writer, and they have two sons, Miles and Oliver. His
work can be viewed online at www.toddtelander.com.